BEGGAR TO BELIEVER

KELLY K

Beggar to Believer by Kelly K
Published by Charisma House, an imprint of Charisma Media
1150 Greenwood Blvd., Lake Mary, Florida 32746

All emphasis in Scripture is the author's own.

Unless otherwise noted, all definitions are from Merriam-Webster.com.

While the author has made every effort to provide accurate, up-to-date source information at the time of publication, statistics and other data are constantly updated. Neither the publisher nor

For more resources like this, visit MyCharismaShop.com.

Cataloging-in-Publication Data is on file with the Library of Congress.
International Standard Book Number: 978-1-63641-556-7
E-book ISBN: 978-1-63641-557-4

1 2025
Printed in the United States of America

Most Charisma Media products are available at special quantity discounts for bulk purchase for sales promotions, premiums, fund-raising, and educational needs. For details, call us at (407) 333-0600 or visit our website at charismamedia.com.

CONTENTS

PART III: LIVE IT OUT

INTRODUCTION

STOP BEGGING—START BELIEVING

HEY, FAMILY! I'M so glad you picked up this book. I believe with all my heart it's not by accident that you're holding *Beggar to Believer* right now. God has something He wants to say to you, and my prayer is that every page shouts His truth louder than the lies of the enemy.

The whole purpose of this book is simple: to help you stop living like a beggar—pleading with God for what He's already promised—and start living like a believer who knows those promises are yours in Christ. This isn't theory, it's not religious fluff, and it's not just another Christian self-help message. It's about shifting your mindset to line up with God's Word so you can finally walk in the freedom, authority, and power Jesus died to give you.

Too many of us love God but still live defeated lives. We pray but don't see answers. We worship but still feel stuck in shame, fear, or lack. We go to church but secretly wonder whether God's promises are for other people and not for us. That's exactly where the enemy wants you to stay—believing *about* God without actually believing *God*. If you've ever felt like your prayers hit the ceiling or your faith isn't producing fruit, then this message is for you. It's time to move from hoping and begging to standing in faith and receiving.

Now I need you to know something right from the start: This book isn't just my story. Yes, you'll hear how God took me from begging Him for scraps to boldly believing His promises. But woven all throughout these chapters are the stories of people just like you—husbands, wives, moms, dads, kids, friends—who grabbed hold of this message and watched God completely flip their lives upside down. They wrote me, they messaged me, they poured out what God was doing, and I knew those testimonies had to be shared. So I'm handing them straight to you in these pages.

And because I want you to see for yourself how real this transformation is, I went one step further. Throughout the book you'll find QR codes you can scan with your phone. These codes will take you to extra content that will encourage you, stretch you, and prove once again that God is still moving in power today. Don't skip them—they're like bonus faith-builders waiting for you!

This book isn't just words on paper. It's an invitation into a journey—a journey from powerless prayers to powerful belief, from begging for God to maybe do something someday to confidently living as a son or daughter who knows their Father keeps His Word.

So let's go! Let's step into this together. As you read, keep your heart open and your Bible close. You're about to see that the shift from beggar to believer doesn't just change your prayer life; it changes everything.

For additional resources, scan the QR code or visit KellyKBooks.com/believer/resources.

PART I

THE BASIC OF BASICS

CHAPTER 1

BELIEF

Belief (noun)

: a state or habit of mind in which trust or confidence is placed in some person or thing

: something that is accepted, considered to be true, or held as an opinion: something believed

BELIEF.

How crazy is it that this one little word can say so much? Six letters to describe millions of lives being saved—or millions of lives being destroyed. Six letters to inspire amazing and beautiful acts of service, gifts of love, and selfless motives. Six letters that have started massive revolutions that changed the world for the better! And even when the change isn't on a global scale, belief in action has led to enormous blessing and change in the lives of individuals as well. All those wonderful things have been accomplished in the name of belief.

On the other hand, many horrible, vile, and straight up malicious acts of hate, rage, and destruction have also been done in the name of belief.

The truth of the matter is this, my friend: Every person in this world is a believer in something. Your beliefs are what drive you every single day. They are the reason you do what you do. Why you dress the way you dress. Why you say what you say. Why you love what you love and hate what you hate. Whether you realize it or not, you live out of—and for—your beliefs.

Sometimes we're conscious of this, but more often than not, we get stuck on autopilot. Someone says something to us, and we react without ever thinking, "Why am I saying this? Why am I doing this?" It's all because we subconsciously live inside the confines of our own beliefs!

But what if? What if we have based our entire lives on a belief that isn't actually true? Or maybe it *is* true, but it's not entirely accurate.

Not a *full* truth? What would that mean? What *could* that mean? If we are consciously or even subconsciously living out of our beliefs, what would that partial truth do to our lives? Think about it.

Now, let's take a time-out for a second. Before we go any further, let's make one thing crystal clear. This book, which you currently hold in your hands, was written specifically for *believers*.

"Come on now, Kelly, you already said we are *all* believers, whether we realize it or not. So that's *all* of us! What's your point?"

I'm specifically talking about people who believe in God—the true God. The Creator of the universe! The God who sent His only Son, Jesus, as a sacrifice for me and you. Oh, and I don't mean simply believing that He *exists*.

Please understand: Believing that God exists is the most basic of basics. This should be the starting point of our belief, not the finish line. In James 2:19 the Bible tells us, "You say you have faith, for you *believe* that there is one God. Good for you! Even the demons *believe* this, and they tremble in terror."

Oh, I love how brutally real and honest the Bible can be! "Good for you that you believe in God!" I can just see James giving a sly smirk, one brow raised, talking out of the side of his mouth with some light, fingertip-to-palm hand clapping near his face. Then his tone shifts. He gets very serious, tilts his head down slightly, and looks you dead in the eye. "But so do demons. And they are so terrified of Him, they tremble in *terror*!"

Wow. Think for a second. What does *your* belief in God stir up in you?

When you say, "I *believe* in God," does that mean you picture an old man in the sky with a big white beard, sending down gifts to those who are good and punishment to those who are bad?

You may be laughing at the absurdity of what I just said; you may be in total agreement with that thought. On the other hand, maybe when you say you believe in God, it means you put your faith totally and completely in His Word. You live by it. You trust it. You know God is leading and guiding your life and your only purpose is to let Him!

Or maybe you are somewhere in between.

Perhaps you are new to all *this stuff*. You believe God is real, but you don't know where to start. Maybe you *used* to believe that He was a good and loving God at one point in your life, but you just aren't sure anymore. I mean, come on, you believed He loved you and had a plan and purpose for you, but then it just didn't play out the way you thought it would. I get it.

The good news is, no matter which one you are, this book is absolutely for you! You at least have the basic of basics down. In our world today, that's not a given. However, if you realize that your belief in God may be exactly that—basic at best—I want you to take a minute and just meditate on James 2:19. (Don't get hung up on the word *meditate*. It just means to think about it.) Think about the weight the verse carries and the greater meaning that's hidden ever so slightly under the surface.

"I say I believe in God, but so do the demons? I've been taught that I am going to heaven simply because I believe. But even God's own enemies believe the same thing I do. I know *they* won't be in heaven. So…?"

Exactly. "So…?"

I need you to get to that point—that place in your mind where you realize that maybe there is more to belief in God than just saying, "I acknowledge God is *real*." Maybe, just maybe, the truth of the matter is that *what* you believe about God is so much more important than simply believing He exists!

This is the hard truth. It took me years to learn this, and eventually it led me to write this book. The hard truth is, *what* you believe about God is consistently affecting every—literally, *every*—single area of your life. Your relationships, your finances, your family, your joy, your peace. Your *everything* is being affected—positively or negatively. It all hinges on what *you believe* about *who* God is and what *His* purpose is for *you*!

Is it starting to sink in yet what a massive role this belief stuff plays in your life?

With that being said, think about it this way: If your personal belief in God and about God is that monumental in every area of your life, maybe it's also a massive bull's-eye on your back for the enemy to zero in on. He holds nothing back, he spares no expense, and he works as hard as possible to deceive you. His goal is to make you believe something false about God, to make you believe God doesn't want you to have or do *exactly* what He does want you to have or do. The enemy's out to steal, kill, and destroy the blessed life God promised you in His Word. Can he do that simply by making you believe you don't deserve it? Or can he even make you believe that it's just not possible?

What if all the devil has to do is alter what you believe—just enough? Just enough that it removes any power your prayers would have carried? I mean, that's the thing about being deceived. Someone who is totally and completely deceived will believe in their heart, 100 percent, that they aren't!

That very scenario is what I see happening all over the world.

I see Christians living lives that are broken and beaten down, just accepting it all as "God's plan." I see men and women all over the world with beautiful hearts for the Father, but they're exhausted and worn out. They give all they have in ministry, to the point of complete burnout. Yet in their own lives, they rarely see or experience the promises God gave to them in the Bible. Does that sound like you?

I see this every day, and it breaks my heart. So I say, "No more!"

God lit a fire in my heart to fight against the lie and the attack of the enemy. I am so over a defeated enemy winning the battle in our minds for what we believe about our God—about who He really is and what He truly wants for us. I won't tolerate that fool's lies for one more minute! We are going to fight back!

To be honest, this is more than that. This is my purpose: to challenge you.

More specifically, my purpose is to challenge your thinking. Because I can't save you. Only Jesus can. I can't change your life. Only Jesus can. I can't even change your thinking. Only Jesus can! My purpose is to show you what a new way of thinking looks like—what Jesus looks like. Who He is, who He *really* is. And just as important, who *you* are once you have given your life to Him.

So if, for some reason, you are reading this book and you can honestly say, "I don't believe there is a God at all," to you I want to say, "What book did you mean to buy instead of this one?" And also, "Hello, I'm Kelly K! I'm so glad you're here!"

I'm teasing of course (but only a little). You may not know why you are here right now. But there is one thing I know: It's not by accident. It's not a coincidence that God is calling you out and speaking directly to you through my words right now. He sees you. He knows you. He has a plan for your life. He *loves* you—so much, in fact, that He made sure this book wound up in your possession. You may not believe in God right now. But oh, son! He believes in you!

I'm not asking you to change your beliefs because of this book. But I *am* asking you to be open and willing to let them be challenged.

So here it is. My challenge to you: Take this journey with me. Let me challenge your thinking. Don't worry, we will use the Word of God as the foundation for it all. Let me show you how transitioning from a beggar mindset to a believer mindset changed everything for me. And it changed everything, not just in my life but also in the lives of my wife and kids and those in my ministry. And I've had the privilege of sharing this life-changing message with millions of other people as well.

I also challenge you to finish what you start. We serve a God of completion! Trust me, if you feel like He wants you to read this book today, He knows what's going to be in it tomorrow. Don't quit halfway. Wait 'til the end to make your final assessment. Your job is simple: Keep an open mind and an open heart—but not to me and my words. Listen to what God is speaking directly to *you* through them.

With that being said, I won't make you take my word for it. I have been sharing the lesson of beggar to believer for years now. And I have been flooded with testimonies from people whose beliefs have been reshaped, whose lives have been changed, and who have started to see power in their prayers like never before. After decades of *begging* God for healing, it just showed up suddenly. Financial breakthroughs arrived apparently overnight. In what felt like an instant, lost children, parents, and friends all came back to Jesus.

So to help with the process, after each chapter, I will include a very true, very real testimony from someone just like you, someone who had to make the same choice being presented to you right now.

The choice? I'm so glad you asked!

You can take the metaphorical blue pill and keep living life as you always have, continuing to get what you've always gotten. Or...

You can take the metaphorical red pill and be open to the fact that there is so much more to who God is and what He truly wants for you and your life. So ask yourself this question: Am I ready? Because once you start this journey, your life is *never* going to be the same again!

Now you have a choice to make, very similar to one I've heard before: "You take the blue pill and the story ends. You wake in your bed and you believe whatever you want to believe.…You take the red pill and you stay in Wonderland and I show you how deep the rabbit-hole goes."[1]

To access more content from Kelly K, scan the QR code or visit KellyKBooks.com/believer/ch1.

JESICA JEWELL

Hi! I want to get this off my heart before I lose the nerve. Kelly asked for testimonies, so here is mine.

I came from a very broken home. I had young parents who just could not get it together. I was in twelve different schools by the time I was in tenth grade. Sometimes I think my parents hated my brother and me more than they hated each other. I suffered multiple forms of abuse, some so terrible that I cannot even bring myself to type the words even now, thirty years later.

My mother was raised in a strict Catholic home, and my father has always been a big "fan" of Jesus. I did not have a clue about religion—just what my grandma taught me. She always said Jesus was my best friend, and as long as I kept Him in my heart and talked to Him about my struggles, He would hear me and see me through it. So all through my early years, no matter what happened or what I endured at whatever age, no matter how terrible or traumatizing it was, I would talk out loud to Jesus. He became my diary and my best friend, even though I did not fully understand. He heard me.

When I was eighteen, I married a man who had his own traumas. He was struggling; *we* struggled. We never stopped fighting. There was so much anger in our home, and I knew it wasn't ours. I knew that the devil was lodged so deep into our lives that we were trapped. For years it felt like we were at war with one another, and I would ask God every day to help me make sense of it all. My husband had never had God in his life.

He was so bitter and angry over the things that had happened to him and the things that he had lost.

We drifted apart, and I honestly was about to give up. I deserved better, my kids deserved better, and *he* deserved better. I pleaded with the Lord; I asked Him to light a path, to wake us up, to pray the ultimate prayer for my family, so to speak, because enough was enough. There was so much pain and so many things we couldn't get past, and no one could help but Him.

I woke up the next morning, and I knew something was different. I could feel it. My husband called me on his way home from work and told me that he had stumbled upon a Christian radio station and he really was thinking about learning more about God. I told him that was a wonderful idea, and it launched everything into full speed right then. He began spending time with the Lord. He spoke to me and to our children differently. Everything began to change.

The final piece to the puzzle came in my struggle with anxiety. Where did I go from here? What's my next move? How was I going to live out loud the truth that I had been trying to beat into everyone else's head? During COVID, I came across one of Kelly's original reels about depression and anxiety in my TikTok For You page. Oh, son! That was it for me. Kelly became my pastor, and y'all became my church family. My husband and I are now subscribed on TikTok, watch Bible study, follow Ryan Edberg Ministries, and watch *Think About THAT for a Minute!* daily. We also both tithe to the ministry every month. I honestly don't know where I would be or where my marriage would be without Pastor Kelly—and, of course, the Almighty Himself.

I decided to send in my story when Kelly spoke about being a friend of Jesus, not a fan. I realized that Jesus was my best friend even before I knew I was doing it right. When I was a little girl just talking out loud, when I needed a friend and was going through it—He was there. I have had a relationship with Him this entire time, even when I felt like I didn't. He came back for the one. That is the most humbling thing I have ever experienced, and I needed to share how Kelly brought me there. I will be eternally grateful. I will never beg Jesus again, and thanks to this family, I can stand firm in my friendship with God. I can't wait to see Jesus continue to move and work in our lives. Thank you, and God bless you all.

CHAPTER 2

THE RED PILL

Same (adjective)
: identical; not different
: exactly like another or each other[1]

Greater (adjective)
: comparative of *great*

Great (adjective)
: of an extent, amount, or intensity considerably above the normal or average[2]
: of ability, quality, or eminence considerably above the normal or average[3]

HEY, HERE YOU are! You did it! You took the red pill. I am so excited for you—for the life you are stepping into. This is literally the first day of the rest of your life!

So back to my earlier question: What if?

What if we have based our entire lives on a belief that isn't actually true? Or, again, maybe it is true, but not entirely accurate. What would *partial truth* mean? If we live out of our beliefs—again, consciously or even subconsciously—what would that do to our lives?

Let's break this down. In the short amount of time we've spent in this book together, we have already learned a few things.

- Belief is powerful and has the ability to enhance life or destroy it.

- Belief drives us, leads us, and, to an extent, can even control us.

This leads us to the obvious conclusion: What we allow ourselves to believe needs to be handled with the utmost importance, care, and reverence, especially when it comes to God.

I mean, think about this for a minute. Your entire walk with God—from the very beginning, straight out of the gate—is all based on only *one* thing. That's right, you read correctly. I said *one.*

"Oh. What is it?"

I am *so* glad you asked! *Belief.* Don't you remember?

For most Christians, if someone asked, "How does a person get saved or give their life to God?" we always send them to the exact same verse, don't we? I mean, you just quoted it in your mind before I even typed it out!

John 3:16.

Now I *know* there is at least one person reading this book right now who just thought, "Hey, I know that one! That's the verse Tim Tebow wrote!" (I kid, I kid.) This isn't a football verse at all. It's not a sports anthem, motto, slogan, or cool bumper sticker. It's the foundation of our faith in Christ.

John 3:16 tells us, "For this is how God loved the world: He gave his one and only Son, so that everyone who *believes* in him will not perish but have eternal life."

Did you catch it? There it is in black and white! Exactly what I've been telling you! God gave His one and only Son as a sacrifice to pay the price, for me and you, so that we could have access to our Father for all eternity. Wow.

Now, here is the kicker. The absolute best and most insane part of this whole thing—our part.

Jesus had to give up His life on this earth for us to have the gift of salvation. It wasn't fun. It wasn't easy. He gave His life for us in the most brutal, painful, and agonizing way imaginable. But He did it! All we have to do to receive it is just *believe.*

Really what I'm trying to show you, in a roundabout way, is that faith is the currency of heaven. Now, read that again.

What that means is that anything you will *ever* need, want, or desire from God will all come the exact same way—by believing it before you ever see it. Believing you will spend an eternity in heaven while you are still on earth. Believing your breakthrough belongs to you before you experience it. Believing your healing is in progress even though the doctors told you it would be impossible. Believing you have more than enough when you can't even afford to pay attention!

Are you starting to get it? Do you see it yet?

I know I'm dragging this out a bit, but I need you to understand why it's not only important but *imperative* that we believe the truth about God—the real truth about who He is, what He promises, and (so very importantly) who you are once you give your life to Him.

Follow me here. Faith is another way of communicating belief. And if faith is the currency of heaven, that means, in simple terms, you receive *from* God what you believe *about* God.

That statement hits harder and is more truthful than you even know—for now.

However, by the time you finish this book, I am fully convinced you will understand why I'm saying that. Let me really open this up for explanation by using another scripture. And this is written in *red* in my Bible!

> I tell you the truth, anyone who believes in me will do the same works I have done, and even greater works, because I am going to be with the Father. You can ask for anything in my name, and I will do it, so that the Son can bring glory to the Father. Yes, ask me for anything in my name, and I will do it!
>
> —John 14:12–14

Oh, son! Did you just read what I just read? In His own words, Jesus just told us that we can do the same things He did—and even *greater*. Wait. What?

Now, before I go any further, let me ask you a few questions:

1. Did you know this verse was in the Bible?

2. Did you know Jesus was talking to *you*? (Not just pastors, preachers, teachers, missionaries, and evangelists. You, yes, *you* can and should do the same things Jesus did, and even greater!)

3. *Are* you doing the same things Jesus did, and even greater?

Right here is where we run into the problem. For most of us, we know this scripture exists. We've read it ourselves and heard it taught in church time and time again. This may be new information to you, and that's totally fine! But if you knew already, it's question three that always seems to stop us dead in our tracks, isn't it? We know the Bible says it. We know Jesus meant it. We understand it was for His disciples at that time, but it also applies to us today. However, when it comes to actually doing it…

Crickets.

Jesus wasn't one to waste words, and He sure wasn't your typical preacher when it comes to exaggerating the point to make more of an impact. He told the truth, the whole truth, and nothing but the truth. More importantly, He meant every word He said.

With that in mind, let's look at some of the wording in this verse again: "I tell you the *truth*, anyone who *believes* in me *will* do the *same* works I have done, *and* even *greater* works, *because* I am going to be with the Father."

I know I added emphasis on multiple words, but is there one in particular sticking out to you like a clown at a funeral? (I don't know whether that's an actual saying or not.) I just want to make sure you catch this. By now, this should be obvious!

"Anyone who *believes* in me will do the same works I have done, and even greater." Right there it is! *Believe.*

Now, before I completely trample all over your salvation and make you feel absolutely awful about yourself, I need you to know that what I am about to show you is in no way meant to bring shame or guilt on you. The Bible says there is *no* condemnation for those who are in Christ. And that's you! But this next part might sting a little. It might make you feel uncomfortable. And that's OK! That's what we need. We have to get out of our comfort zones. Trust me on this—I won't leave you in shambles for long, I promise.

Here is what you have to see, not only physically but spiritually. Remember what John 3:16 told us? "Everyone who *believes* in him will not perish but have eternal life."

What did it take to receive your salvation? You know, that gift Jesus died to give you? That gift that we could never afford, pay for, attain, or acquire on our own? What did it take for you to gain access to the Father and eternity in paradise forever?

Oh yeah. Belief.

All you and I have to do is believe. Believe that Jesus is the Son of God. Believe that Jesus lived a perfect life, free of *all* sin. Believe that He gave up that life as a sacrifice for us on the cross. Believe that He didn't stay dead! Believe that He rose out of that tomb after three days, just like He told us He would. Believe that Jesus, who had no sin, became our sin so that you and I, who had no right standing with God, could enter right standing with God.

I'm trying to lead you into it. Have you made the connection yet? If not, buckle up, buttercup—here we go!

The belief you needed to receive your salvation is the *exact* same belief Jesus was talking about in John 14:12.

In John 3:16 Jesus tells us that to be saved, we just have to believe. Then in John 14:12 He says that anyone who *believes* in

Him *will* do the same works He did, and even *greater*! I'm going to let that sink in for a second.

You good to move on? Are you putting the pieces together? I hope so. Because we are just getting started. There's more.

Why is it that so many Christians have no problem with believing to receive their salvation, but when it comes time for them to pray for someone to be healed—"Well, I don't know about all that."

Are you kidding me?

The belief it took to get you saved is the *same* belief it takes to pray for the blind to have their eyes opened. The belief it took to get you saved is the same belief it takes for you to walk up to a stranger in the grocery store and give them a word directly from God, through you, that speaks straight to their circumstance and brings them peace. The belief it took to get you saved is the same belief it takes for you to tell the mountain in your life to get up and move, and it *has* to obey.

Do you see? Are the pieces falling into place? If so, you may have beaten me to the punch!

When you claim to be a Christian and say you believe in Jesus for salvation, that should also mean that you are doing the same things Jesus did, and even greater. Because that's precisely what Jesus said.

John 14:12 doesn't say, "Anyone who believes in me *might* do the same things I have done, and even greater." It doesn't say, "Anyone who believes in me *could possibly* do the same things I have done, and even greater." What Jesus said was, "Anyone who believes in me *will* do the same things I have done, and even greater."

This isn't optional. It's a requirement!

In the previous chapter, we saw that the demons believe in God. They even believe Jesus is the Son of God. So what's the difference? What sets *us* apart from *them*? How can you tell between someone who, just on a basic level, believes God exists and someone who has truly put all their faith and hope in their belief in Him?

Easy. You will be able to tell them apart because everywhere they go, they bring joy. Peace. Love. People get set free. People get healed. You will know who they are because they do the same things Jesus did, and even greater.

Ouch. I know. That was my reaction when I first got this revelation as well.

Miracles follow those who follow the One in charge of the miracles! Having the Holy Spirit in your life without seeing miracles happen everywhere you go is like hearing "Don't Stop Believing" by Journey on the radio, and you *don't* sing along. It's impossible.

Essentially, what I am telling you (just in case it hasn't been made crystal clear already) is this: How can we say we truly believe for salvation when we can't believe for all the rest? The power stuff? If it really is the exact same belief and we aren't doing the same things Jesus did—are we really saved?

To access more content from Kelly K, scan the QR code or visit KellyKBooks.com/believer/ch2.

DONNA FERRAN

For many years I was walking around seeking fulfillment in others. I was in *horrible* relationships for far too long because I was trying to fill that void. When those relationships brought me down further, I'd drink alcohol multiple times a week to try to numb those feelings. I was hurt from past relationships, I was hurt when my children didn't do things the way that helped me feel loved, I was hurt when I felt left out—I was just hurt.

One day I was scrolling through TikTok and came across Kelly. He

taught me how to pray differently and say thank you instead of begging. He taught me that Jesus already paid for it all on the cross. My prayer life changed, and I started thanking God for everything. I became a believer instead of a beggar. God has since filled that void that *was* inside me. I realized I was missing Him and that all I need is Him. His love has filled every void, and I lack for nothing now. I see things that hurt me before through a Jesus lens now, and they don't hurt anymore.

My desires have completely changed since I opened up my heart to Him and started thanking Him. I love our daily studies and going to the physical church I attend. I'm reading and understanding the Bible, I've attended a Power and Love conference, I listen to Christian music day and night, I don't care to touch alcohol anymore, I love and long to be the hands and feet of Jesus, and I've even signed up to get baptized in June. I hunger for God, His Word, and His guidance. His love fulfills me and gives me joy and peace that only He can provide.

I am so grateful for that fateful day I found Kelly and for the day he taught me how to say *thank You* in prayer! Being a believer instead of a beggar has turned my world inside out in the best possible way.

CHAPTER 3

GET RID OF THAT STINKIN' THINKIN'!

Permeate (verb)

: to diffuse through or penetrate something

: to pass through the pores or interstices of

LET ME START this chapter with a *very* sincere apology. I am so sorry! If I could give you a big hug right now, I would!

I know that was a cruel way to end the previous chapter. In the famous words of Stephanie Tanner, "How rude!" I do believe, however, it was a "necessary evil." We all need wake-up calls like that at some point in our walk with God. Honestly, we need them regularly. Throughout our relationship with Him, we need times when we are forced to evaluate what God's Word *actually* says. We need to see it in black and white for ourselves. We need to make sure we are following His plan to the best of our ability.

Now let's address the question that threw us into spiritual shock at the end of the previous chapter. I promised you I wouldn't leave you in metaphorical pieces for long. And I am, if nothing else, a man of my word.

"Are we really saved?"

Yes, a thousand times, yes! We are *really* saved! I posed the question because we need moments in our lives that challenge us. Those moments prove our trust in Him is still valid, still credible, and most of all, still essential. It's just way too easy for us to forget what the Bible tells us about how God works.

> "My thoughts are nothing like your thoughts," says the Lord. "And my ways are far beyond anything you could imagine. For just as the heavens are higher than the earth, so my ways are higher than your ways and my thoughts higher than your thoughts."
>
> —Isaiah 55:8–9

Now back to the matter at hand. We can't move on before laying down a little more foundation.

Never forget: Our salvation is *all* about the *belief* part. It's not the works we do or don't do. Those are good, but they're not where salvation comes from. Jesus loves us unconditionally, and He paid for our eternity selflessly, not for what He could get out of us in return. If you truly believe in your heart that Jesus is the Son of God and He gave His life to pay for your sins so that you could spend eternity with Him and His Father, you absolutely will!

However, if we look at the cross and see *only* a "ticket to heaven," we've missed it. What Jesus bought and paid for on the cross was so much more than that! But we will dive into that a little later.

We know we are still going to make it to heaven even if we don't put ourselves out there to be used as a vessel for God. You know, like He *literally* told us to. (You can thank Jesus for that!) But time-out. Let's address this "stinkin' thinkin'" before it permeates our entire lives. Our lives should be a "Christ-like fragrance rising up to God" (2 Cor. 2:15).

If, for some reason, you have a thought forming along the lines of, "Whew, thank God! I am so glad I don't *have* to do all…that! And I still get to go to heaven? Well, praise God!"—that's the wrong mindset too. Frankly, it stinks. And to be brutally honest, it's an ignorant mindset. It's a *selfish* mindset. It's a castle mindset, not a kingdom mindset. (We will talk about that in chapter 22.)

Let me show you.

When God asks us to do something, we tend to focus on the *what* part of His request. If *what* He asked me to do sounds fun, fits my schedule, and is something I wanted to do anyway—sure, I'm all in! Yet when what He asks doesn't sound fun, doesn't fit my schedule, and isn't something I want to do—well, that's a different story, isn't it?

But God's not like us, is He?

I mean, we are created in His image. So we are like Him. But He is most certainly not like us, not in the sense of what *drives* us, anyway. We are motivated by reciprocation: the promise of reward or personal gain. For the most part, we do what we do so we can get what we want.

Maybe that's the problem: It's what *we* want.

On the other hand, what does God want? Why does He do what He does? What does He want out of the tasks He gives us and the sacrifices He asks us to make? The answer probably won't surprise you at all.

People. God cares about people. He cares about *us*.

But even deeper than that, and more importantly, He cares about our hearts—the position and posture of our hearts. Our attitudes. The motive that lives deep inside every one of us. The hidden motive that no one truly knows. Well, no one but you—and Him.

Over many years of getting to know God personally and spending time in His Word daily, I've come to learn that almost everything He has ever done and will ever do is always connected to the *why* behind the ask rather than the *what* it takes to accomplish it.

Now let's dig deep.

To access more content from Kelly K, scan the QR code or visit KellyKBooks.com/believer/ch3.

DONNA BOURGEOIS

I was unemployed for five months. I watched Kelly's lives every day. I would put in requests for prayer that I would find a job. One day, last January, Kelly mentioned during a live that God told him that someone was desperately looking for a job, and that God was going to bless them with not just one but two jobs—and the second job would not only be better than the first one, but it would also be something they'd never expect. I thought to myself, "That's got to be me." I applied for two jobs that day, and I was hired the next week.

Yes, God loves me, and I loved my new job! But it only lasted six weeks before there were layoffs. From there I struggled financially, with money running out. Again, I continued to beg God every day for a job and asked for prayer on every live and on the Facebook group, and I asked my dad to pray for me.

Two months later, I got the opportunity to test for the company I'd always wanted to work for. This was it. On my way to my test, God spoke to me for the first time: "Come work for Me." I started to laugh and cry. I thought, "OK, God, I will."

Because I was too obsessed with my test, I bombed it and later wondered what God was talking about. I kept my pace and continued begging. There was one more place to apply, but I needed two more welding tickets to qualify. Testing day came, and what should have been an easy test was not. My test plate snapped in two pieces. Devastated, I left immediately for home, sobbing uncontrollably, feeling like a failure with nowhere else to go, job-wise.

I called the prayer line for help and bawled the whole time. I just needed some comfort—to feel some peace. I'm not sure I even listened to the person praying for me, but I did start to hear the peaceful tone of the person. I pulled off the highway into a parking lot and prayed by myself after this phone call.

"OK, God, I've got nothing left. I'm tired of fighting to find a job. I'm exhausted. It's all You now. I'm going to rest in You."

I went online to look for people to pray for, thinking that if I put my thoughts, focus, and prayers on others, it would help me forget my struggle to find a job. Later that day, a thought came to me about a job I saw with the same company I had been pursuing. It wasn't welding, but any income would've been great at that point. I was down to my last hundred dollars. On Monday, I got an email from this company for a laborer job to work at the shipyard where I had failed my welding test.

It has now been four months working at the shipyard, and I do mostly tank watch, which is not labor intensive. I make twelve dollars more per hour than the first job I got last January, doing something I never expected and working for the employer I really wanted. You see, I heard God's voice to go to work for Him, but I didn't let go of the reins until complete failure. I needed to truly rest in Him and believe He loved me so much that He would rescue me from my despair.

He had a plan all along—I just prolonged it. I always thought I had great faith before, but this showed me what faith and believing was all about! I walk into that building every day in awe that my God is so good and gave me this job, and I have the biggest smile on my face. He had a plan for me all along!

CHAPTER 4

IT'S ABOUT THE *WHY*—NOT THE *WHAT*

Trust (noun)

: assured reliance on the character, ability, strength, or truth of someone or something

: one in which confidence is placed

WHEN GOD ASKS us to do something, it's not always about the specific act or action. It's because of the *why* behind it. There's always a motive. A goal. A purpose. We just can't always see it. It's like it's just below the surface, completely out of sight to us—but it makes total and complete sense to God. We just need to *trust* Him.

For example, let's say you are reading your Bible one morning, and God speaks to you! He gives you a brand-new understanding of a scripture you were reading, one you have read for years but never really understood.

Right at that moment, when you start to feel that supernatural peace and joy—the kind that comes only from knowing you just had God Himself speak to you—He speaks again! But this time He says, "Make a video about what I just taught you, and post it online for others to see."

"Um, nope. Hard pass!"

Because you already know, right? You know the Internet is a cruel and vicious wasteland of trolls, bullies, and joy bandits.

People on the Internet are *mean*, son! (And I'm not just talking about the "lost" people far from God. The Christians can be just as brutal, if not worse, at times!)

"Hard pass, God! Thank You for giving me this new revelation and understanding. But, uh, I say we let a sleeping dog lie. Let's not mess up a good thing, God, You know what I mean? Let's let this one be...something special. You know, for just You and me."

That sounds reasonable, right? Godly even. But where is the focus? More importantly, *who* is the focus?

You. Me. Us. And was that ever the point to *any* of this?

When God offered you the gift of salvation, wasn't your life the *first* thing He asked you to lay down? To give it up? To no longer live for what *you* want? Isn't that the entire point of all this? To let Him live through you?

Exactly.

We are so focused on how we are going to feel or look—or what it's going to cost—if we do what God wants that we lose sight of the greater purpose. His purpose. My life is not my own anymore. I gave it to God. He is the main character of my story. Not me. He gets the glory. Not me!

I'm not the lead in my own story anymore. I gave up that role the moment I gave Him my life. I'm not the star—I'm the supporting cast. He writes the script. He directs the action. And He gets the credit.

Oh, by the way, the same goes for you!

When God asked me to start sharing online what He was teaching me in His Word, initially all I could see was me. *My* feelings. *My* fears. *My* reputation. *My* follower count. Yeah, you get it. I could only see how this affected me. However, in that very moment, while I was looking at the cost of today, God was *years* ahead of me, looking at the reward! I saw hateful comments, mean tweets, lost friends, and unsubscribes. God saw souls—lives changed forever. He saw eternal relationships with His most precious children that otherwise could have been stolen from Him by the enemy.

Talk about a mind shift!

Just like you had no idea, at first, that this was actually a true story about how my ministry came into existence, I had no idea what God was about to do with something as simple as, "Make a video and post it on the Internet."

How could I? How could I know that *that* video was about to be the start of something? Something big. Something that went so far beyond me, I will *never* know the full reach, not on this side of heaven, anyway. I saw an interruption in my day and an irritation to my comfort. God saw a worldwide ministry! God saw marriages being restored, bodies being healed, minds being renewed, chains of addiction and depression being broken off individuals and families forever.

God saw a future that I wouldn't have believed if He told me. God saw more than just a single video about what He showed me one time. God saw a daily, live, online *church*! He saw a day coming when over one hundred people would give their hearts and lives to Him though this ministry every single day! Wow.

But isn't that how it always goes? Doesn't He *always* outsee our extremely limited vision? I mean, let's be real. This should actually bring a whole new level of peace into your life. You don't have to worry about anything! God has already gone before you and made a way (Deut. 31:8).

We just need to get to the point where we truly understand that obedience is always worth it. We have to trust Him.

I know, I know—easier said than done. Or maybe not. After all, we're still just creasing the cover on this bad boy!

To access more content from Kelly K, scan the QR code or visit KellyKBooks.com/believer/ch4.

BARBARA BEVER

Glory be to the almighty God! I always believed in Jesus, but I never felt the same way that saved people *looked*. You know, that joy on their faces and peace in their actions. I never felt loved and protected by a higher authority. I prayed, "God, please. God, if You notice me and if it be Your will"—the typical "beggar" stuff. It felt more like wishing than knowing it was heard.

God answered prayers for me even though I did not deserve it, and instead of calling it blessed, I would say, "Wow, that was amazing *luck*." I went to church and heard the Scriptures, but never once did they explain what they meant. It didn't make me feel any closer to God; it just made me feel like I knew less than I did before and ashamed of who I am: a woman. They didn't preach ways to lift women up in Christ. They said that as a woman I am lesser because women can cause men to sin. It left me feeling worthless—why would God *ever* want me? So I left the church.

As the years went by, I felt depressed, alone, unloved, and burdened by all the weight on my shoulders. I married, had children, divorced, married, and divorced again. God wasn't in my marriages, so they failed horribly. Now I'm sixty, and one night I was mindlessly scrolling, and I started to see videos explaining the meaning behind different Bible stories. All of a sudden, I was thirsty for more. So I kept scrolling until I came across Kelly K's shorts. Without a doubt, I believe God was leading me to Kelly.

I listened to one after another of his videos for over eight hours. Because Kelly is so passionate and fiercely in love with God, I was drawn by the passion for our Father and His holy words. Each episode he would ask, "Are you willing to pay the full price? Are you willing to give up everything—your heart, your thoughts, your wants and desires? Are you willing to be dead to this world and keep your *eyes on God*?"

Praise His holy name, God hit me like a Mack truck! I confessed all the sins that I could remember. Let me tell you, I felt such shame having to repeat everything. But then *pure peace* and *joy* overcame me.

I actually feel God's love! I hear the Holy Spirit speak to me. I have been cleansed and paid for. I listen to an audio Bible during work, and it plays a movie in my head. I have been saved for about five months, and every workday for eight to ten hours I am listening to the Bible, except when I listen to Kelly.

God has blessed me with sleep. He has blessed me with four house payments. He blessed me with the desire to talk about Him. I am so blessed to be able to talk to God, knowing He and Jesus can hear me. In my prayers I always thank Him for never giving up on me. My most comforting scripture is John 10:28–29.

All glory to God forever and ever. Amen, amen, amen.

CHAPTER 5

THE BIBLE IS A MOSAIC

Miss the Forest for the Trees (idiom)

: to not understand or appreciate a larger situation, problem, etc., because one is considering only a few parts of it

: to be unable to get a general understanding of a situation because you are too worried about the details[1]

I HOPE THIS IS starting to stir your faith. I hope there's at least a flicker—a fresh ember smoldering on the inside of your heart. More specifically, I hope there's a new *desire* in your heart. A desire that didn't originate from you. A desire for more. To know more. To go deeper. Is that starting to sound like you? If not, just wait. It's coming!

So what is the why behind the what in John 14:12? "I tell you the truth, anyone who believes in me will do the same works I have done, and even greater works, *because* I am going to be with the Father."

And there it is! Plain as day! "*Because* I am going to be with the Father."

"Uh, OK, Kelly. What does that even mean?"

Oh, I am so glad you asked! For all this to come full circle, let's move forward a few verses. In John 14:15–17, Jesus says,

> If you love me, obey my commandments. And I will ask the Father, and he will give you another Advocate, who will never leave you. He is the Holy Spirit, who leads into

> all truth. The world cannot receive him, because it isn't looking for him and doesn't recognize him. But you know him, because he lives with you now and later will be in you.

Are you starting to see it? A couple of chapters later, in John 16:7, Jesus tells us, "It is best for you that I go away, because if I don't, the Advocate won't come. If I do go away, then I will send him to you."

You see, the Bible is a mosaic. You can't zoom in too close. You'll miss the forest for the trees. I don't even have to tell you to trust me on this. You already know. This happens—a lot.

We need to make sure that when we read the Bible, we understand each scripture as it is *intended* to be understood—in the context of the complete and total fullness of His Word. When we don't, that's taking scriptures out of context. When we isolate a verse from its surrounding verses, chapter, and broader context, we might end up believing a false truth about Scripture. And that, my friend, is an extremely dangerous thing to do when it comes to the Word of God. I mean, can you even build a solid belief on a fractured, unstable foundation?

For example, Philippians 4:13 (NKJV). The verse, "I can do all things through Christ who strengthens me," is often used as motivation for success in our own personal lives and desires. We also consider this scripture the ultimate "pump up" verse. Sports stars in every arena will wear it proudly on their helmets, shoes, shirts, and even under their eyes. But its true meaning, what God is actually teaching us, is about our ability to endure hardships through our faith in Him.

Yeah, not the same at all.

That leads us to John 14:15–17 and John 16:7. Both explain Jesus' reason for leaving the earth and returning to the Father: so that you and I can have access to the Holy Spirit! Jesus tells us, "It's good that I'm on earth, but it's even *better* if I leave!"

What? Time-out! Does that even make sense? "It's *better* if You leave, Jesus? I do *not* agree! Look at all the people You could heal! There are so many men, women, and children You could help! We need You here, Jesus!" That's probably what most of us would think, right?

Let's try thinking differently for a moment. How many people are on the planet right now? Well, according to Siri, 8.2 billion people in 2025—every single one of them with a need that only Jesus can meet. Now let's do some math.

If there are roughly 8.2 billion people on earth, that means that for Jesus to spend just *one* hour with each person, it would take 8.2 billion hours! I mean, even if Jesus spent only one second with each person, that would still equate to about 260 years!

Have you figured it out already? It would be impossible. That's why it's better if He leaves. Because then He gets to send us the Holy Spirit.

And oh, son! I'm not talking about a dialed-down version either. We get the real deal! The Holy Spirit that Jesus had while He was on earth is the exact same Holy Spirit you and I have living inside us right now! If that doesn't put a smile on your face, a spring in your step, and joy in your heart—son, I don't know what will!

I think you are starting to get it, but let's remove any doubt. Jesus went to be with the Father—that's the what. The why behind it is so you and I could get the Holy Spirit. But not "just because." Not just for fun. There is a *purpose* for us receiving the Holy Spirit. And the truth of this very real situation can be a tough pill to swallow. Many Christians never actually get that far. They never get to the why behind their new "roommate" and friend. That's a problem. And I'll show you why.

How was Jesus able to perform all the miracles and signs and wonders that He did? Through the power of the Holy Spirit (Acts 2:22). And what did He say we would do if we believed in Him? The same things, and even greater! And why would Jesus expect something so seemingly ridiculous from us? He doesn't!

He doesn't expect *you* to heal anyone. He doesn't expect *you* to save anyone. He doesn't expect *you* to do *any* of the heavy lifting at all! He doesn't have to. He knows the Holy Spirit will. Miracles and signs and wonders are kind of His thing!

What Jesus does expect, however, is that we honor our end of the deal—our part of the contract, if you will. You remember, don't you?

> Then, calling the crowd to join his disciples, he said, "If any of you wants to be my follower, you must give up your own way, take up your cross, and follow me."
>
> —Mark 8:34

Jesus showed His love, dedication, and commitment to us by giving up His life on the cross. And what exactly are the terms and conditions of the agreement He made with us? Oh, nothing crazy or anything. You know, just to do the same things He did. That's all.

Yeah—that's all.

The reason we will do the same things Jesus did—and even greater—is because we have the same Holy Spirit that He has. Because we gave up our lives. We made a trade—one that tilted entirely in our favor, but a trade nonetheless. We trade in our plans, desires, and motives in exchange for a *relationship* with the Father, and all *eternity* in paradise with Him.

And since I no longer live for my own desires, and the only plans I have are to be the hands and feet of Jesus, the only logical, reasonable, and truly honoring response to my belief in Him—and to this agreement we made—is to *do the same things Jesus did*!

Because *I'm* not the one doing it at all. The Holy Spirit is!

The only thing I should want is what Jesus wants. And what does Jesus want? For us to examine His life in Scripture, pay close attention to what He did and why He did it, and go do the same things.

Oh yeah—and even *greater*.

To access more content from Kelly K, scan the QR code or visit KellyKBooks.com/believer/ch5.

DAN THIEL

Kelly, I have been told for years I need to share my testimony, so here it goes.

In reality my whole life is my testimony. The fact that I'm alive at all is evidence of God's greatness. The number of close calls and dumb things I made Him rescue me from—and my journey back to Him—have been incredible.

I was raised in the Catholic Church and was very involved. I got confirmed early to teach and lead youth. Then my grandfather passed away when I was sixteen. He was the man who taught me to ride horses, and he went to church twice a week—but he was Lutheran. When I brought it up to the priest, I was told he was in purgatory. I was rightfully upset. Long story short, I was asked not to come back to the church. So I didn't. For the next six years, I lived my life in and of the world: chewing tobacco, drinking, and smoking.

My first close call was all *Survivor*'s fault. As a child of the '90s, my buddies and I were obsessed with that show. We decided we were a bunch of hillbillies, so we could probably win. Thus, "survivor week" was born. Two of my buddies and I camped on the local riverbank for a week every summer. No food, no tent—just fishing poles, .22 rifles, and whatever illicit substances we could scrounge up.

The summer before my senior year was the worst. We went the first two days without killing or catching a single thing to eat. The third morning, I decided I was going to find some form of food, so I threw my line in the water and started walking down the riverbank. I ended up finding a timber rattler under a rock. I pinned its head down, cut the head off, tried to cook it on a spit, and ate it. According to the local hospital, I most likely cut the venom glands in half and basically glazed the meat with venom while cooking it.

On top of that, it gave me a nasty viral infection. I spent the first

three months of my senior year in the hospital with fevers as high as 107.3, while the doctors told my parents that, the infection being viral, my body would either learn to fight it, or it wouldn't. As I began to recover, they ran tests to make sure nothing was permanently damaged, and the only thing they came up with was that my pancreas was functioning at only about 85 percent of normal. But they had no previous numbers for comparison, so they weren't worried.

My time in the Navy had a profound ability to make all my bad habits significantly more entrenched. I did some dumb stuff on a motorcycle, but otherwise I just did my time and got out. At the end of 2012, I moved to Ohio, met my wife, and never left.

Just after our wedding, I decided two hundred pounds wasn't OK. I had always been a pretty athletic guy, so I started to diet. I cut out soda and a few other things and dropped forty pounds in a month and a half. Then came the day at work when I had to weld all day. We would take turns welding inside a vessel for fifteen minutes at a time. After the umpteenth stint, I came out and basically passed out. My supervisor sent me to urgent care, and after some testing, I got the news: "You're diabetic." Turns out my pancreas was slowly dying all that time.

So there I was: a struggling newlywed with a drinking problem, an almost constant tobacco chewer, and a diabetic.

After a few discussions, my wife and I decided to find a church to go to and found Sebring Friends Church. I won't lie—it was the pastor's *Duck Dynasty* beard that hooked me. I had grown up in a "nicest clothes only" Catholic church, and here was a pastor whose office had turkey fans and deer heads on the walls. I was home. I decided I was done drinking, got baptized again, and rededicated my life to Christ in the spring of 2016.

Life was great, until I fell off the willpower wagon. I relapsed only once. I drank until I blacked out. I got home—enough of a blessing in itself. Then I got into a fight with my wife about how much better she could do and how I didn't deserve anything but her divorcing me. She said that wasn't an option. So I got my pistol out of the bedside table and tried to shoot myself. Somehow, drunkenly, I missed. I only managed to put a hole in our ceiling. The next day, I checked into a Celebrate Recovery program, and by the Lord's hand, I haven't had a drink since.

My latest close call was in April 2021, when I was well into my walk with Christ. I was working on an industrial saw and got caught in it. My arm was pulled in, and a decent amount of the skin was removed. By the protection of Jesus alone, I kept the arm and all the function of my hand and limb. Had one thing been different, my life would have been permanently changed.

Now, by God's grace and my wife's determination, neither of which I deserve, I have a wonderful, Christ-centered family. Kelly, my oldest, actually dreams of working for you one day (you'll have to wait a bit—she is just about to turn eight). But if you ever need a divinely protected electrician, let me know.

CHAPTER 6

THE GREAT COMMISSION

Commission (noun)

: an instruction, command, or duty given to a person or a group of people[1]

: a group of people officially charged with a particular function[2]

DON'T SAY IT, don't say it, don't say it! I already know what you're thinking. "Kelly, seriously. Why do you keep showing us that we will do the same things Jesus did and even greater, but you keep avoiding the most *insane* part of that statement? How could we ever do anything that would be considered *greater* than what Jesus did?"

Now *that* is a great question.

I had to wait until now. You wouldn't still be here if I had just shot straight out of the gate with, "This book will teach you how to do miracles greater than Jesus did!" I'd hope not, anyway. And if I ever actually *do* say something like that, run!

I needed to start changing your thinking on a smaller scale first. We had to build a solid foundation—one that you could see for yourself and know is secure. Now you understand how important *what* you believe is. Let's pair that up with the truth about what it means to believe in Jesus. Now we can start building at a much faster rate!

So what are the *greater* works?

That really is the million-dollar question, isn't it? I mean, come on! How could Jesus say something like that? "Greater works?

Than *You,* Jesus? Seriously?" If I stepped up to the pulpit next Sunday and told the congregation, "I expect you to do something *greater* than Jesus did this week," I'd be at the unemployment office on Monday. Right? Why did Jesus say it then? If we think that's heresy and it's wrong to even think such a thing, what was the point of putting it in the Bible?

This is part of our problem. We have to start asking the *right* questions.

Where is the focus?

"If *we* think..." "How could *we* ever..."

"I expect *you* to do something greater."

You got it! On us.

How easy it is for us to renege on our arrangement so quickly! In the blink of an eye, the very life we gave up to Jesus is now back in our possession and has hijacked our focus. This is why the Bible tells us we need to renew our minds *daily* to the Word of God (Rom. 12:2).

Was Jesus saying that He expects *us* to perform bigger, better, more spectacular miracles than He did? Of course not! We aren't the ones who do miracles *at all*! It's the Holy Spirit who now works through all of us!

All of us (John 14:10, 16–17). Did it just click? I hope so!

Imagine back to the day Jesus first said those famous words in John 14. Now let's say that once He finishes preaching, Jesus decides to take all His disciples out to dinner. They start out on their journey to Chick-fil-A to celebrate an epic day of preaching. But when they get to the restaurant, there is a sign on the door that reads, "No shirt, no shoes, no Holy Spirit, *no service*!"

Let me give you a fourth-grade math equation. Out of a party of thirteen, how many will be seated?

Exactly! One. Jesus was the only One with the Holy Spirit.

He hadn't gone to the Father yet. So those who believed in Him didn't have the power of the Holy Spirit inside them—yet.

There is only one Jesus, my friend. But there are 8.2 *billion* of us.

"Now, Kelly, come on—you know better!"

I know, I know—8.2 billion is the number of people on the planet, not the number of people who have the Holy Spirit. (For now!)

Isn't it just the next logical connection to make? We will do greater works than Jesus did because there is a greater number of believers who carry with them the Holy Spirit? Why does *greater* have to mean *better*? Or even *bigger*? What if it meant *more*? The word translated "greater works" is *megas*, and it can be used to convey a number or quantity that is "numerous, large, abundant."[3]

Let me show you something else. In Acts 1:8 we get what is known as the Great Commission. This is the final assignment Jesus gave to us while He was on earth.

> But you will receive power when the Holy Spirit comes upon you. And you will be my witnesses, telling people about me everywhere—in Jerusalem, throughout Judea, in Samaria, and to the ends of the earth.
>
> —Acts 1:8

"Hold up there, Kelly. Let me get this straight. Is this verse telling us that we need to go to the Middle East and start witnessing?"

No! Not at all!

I'll be honest with you. I don't really believe that you actually thought that. But I needed you to see it to make two points:

1. We can't get hung up on the *where* part of the verse. Let's think of it like this: Jerusalem = Your city or town. Judea = Your state. Samaria = Your country. The ends of the earth = The whole world! What Jesus is communicating is that it's *our* job to *go* and *tell* everyone!

2. Jesus didn't tell us to go witness. He said, "And you will *be* my witnesses."

Jesus used the word *witness* as a noun. So why do we always use it as a verb? "We're going to go witness to people at the park today!" "I got to witness to a guy at work last week." "Somebody needs to go witness to Karen; she needs Jesus." If we use the word *witness* as a verb, it tells us what to do. If we use the word *witness* as a noun, it tells us who we are.

The Bible is a mosaic. Remember? If we zoom out of Acts 1:8 and pair it up with John 14:12, our mission on this earth starts to become painfully obvious.

You see, I think Jesus knew. I think He knew, even way back then, the bad habits we would have today. For one, if we don't feel like we have all the information first, we just won't do something. Any excuse to get out of a responsibility, right? Netflix isn't going to watch itself! I think Jesus knew that if He didn't tell us specifically *where* to do the same things He did, and even greater, we just wouldn't do them. After all, how can we be expected to know what God wants?

So He just puts it out there. Pure and simple.

What would that sound like today, I wonder? In my mind, I hear it kind of like this: "OK, boys, you're about to receive the power! The same power I have. But this power is actually attached to a person—the Holy Spirit. Now, get ready! When the Holy Spirit shows up in your life, you are going to see some *stuff*! Pay attention to the stuff He does—what He does through you, sure, but also what He *speaks* to you! Pay close attention.

"Then go tell the people! But don't just *tell* them—*show* them. Start here, in your hometown. Then go further. Tell the whole state! But don't stop there. Why don't you just tell the whole country? And when you finish with that, tell every single person in the entire *world*!

"Tell them about *Me*. Show them what I am all about. If you encounter any demons along the way, tell them they *have* to leave. Use My name when you do! That *always* works! Lay your hands on the sick, and tell them to be healed. Don't worry; they *will* recover. Your name isn't on the line anyway. Mine is. So don't worry about what happens; just trust Me. Oh yeah, and one more thing. Tell them I'm coming back."

Wow.

How can we be expected to know what God wants? Simple. He told us.

Does it still seem so ridiculous to believe that we can do the same things Jesus did and even greater? I don't think that sounds unreasonable! And all we had to do to get here was change the way we *think*. Are you starting to feel it yet? The weight? The burden that comes with truly knowing what God is asking us to do?

In Matthew 11:30, Jesus said, "For my yoke is easy to bear, and the burden I give you is light."

Jesus never said we wouldn't have to carry *any* of the weight. He just said it won't be too heavy! Why do so many people hold on to the belief that "free gift of salvation" means "nothing required"?

Pretty soon we will dig deeper into exactly what the burden is that we need to carry. For now, I just want you to feel it. To at least acknowledge it's there. To reach the point where you start to think, "Could there be more? More than just getting into heaven? More than just suffering through this life, waiting for something great in the next? More that God wants to do in me? More that God wants to do *through* me? Could there be *more*?"

Ask the Holy Spirit yourself. Today. Right now! Don't wait 'til we finish this book! Ask Him, "What do *You* want to do through *me*?" Then listen—and move!

This is where *greater* starts!

To access more content from Kelly K, scan the QR code or visit KellyKBooks.com/believer/ch6.

CRYSTAL RODDENBERRY

When I first started watching Kelly, I was not in the game of praying on the regular. I had just gotten away from a crazy ex-boyfriend. I had to deal with the court system to put him in prison. And I had finally come out of homelessness with my three kids. Many things, like anxiety and fear, had become a part of my daily life because of all the things I had been through with my ex-boyfriend in the past two years. These spirits were huge when I was driving places. I hated being late, I was nervous about who I would see, and I was scared that his family would retaliate. I live in a pretty small town, so running into his family was a huge daily possibility. I became self-isolated and rarely left my home.

Here is where prayer changed all this. When I first heard Pastor Kelly teach on praying like a believer, not a beggar, I thought it sounded silly. Thank Him first? How can that make sense? But I decided to give it a whirl.

I remember so vividly the first time I truly *felt* the change. I was heading to pick up my eldest from the bus stop, and I was running late. I had to get the baby ready, and we weren't going to be there on time. I was frazzled, rushing, anxious, and stressed out. I got in the driver's seat, started the car, and began to back out. Pastor Kelly had taught that those feelings aren't of the Lord, so I decided to give the believer-not-a-beggar thing a try. As I started driving down the road, I said, "Thank You, Lord, for removing this anxiety, this fear and stress I have. I trust You and put my drive in Your hands. Amen."

As soon as I said amen, I instantly felt a wave of calm, peace, and ease come over me. The fear of not making it on time—*gone*. The worry that I wasn't going to have a place to park—*silenced*. My nerves that were making me shake and have a knot in my stomach—*not there*! It was instant, and I have not looked back since. Oh, and yes, I made it on time to pick him up—of course I did!

Now sometimes I start to say, "Please, will You..." but then I mindfully change my words to those of a believer, not a beggar. It has made a difference in many areas of my life, and I'm so thankful for the beggar-to-believer teaching!

CHAPTER 7

BELIEF THAT *AMAZED*

Moot Point (idiom)

: a point or claim that doesn't matter[1]

: a fact that does not apply to the current situation[2]

I HOPE YOU ARE starting to see now that your belief is powerful, not only in that it contains power but also in that it comes with its own power source: the Holy Spirit! We don't have to create the power; we just need to keep it *charged.*

Now what I want to do is start to fine-tune that belief. Give it direction. Action. Aim. Jesus always hit the bull's-eye, and that should be our goal as well. When He spoke, His words went straight to the heart. And when He prayed—oh, son! There was *power.* Everywhere Jesus went, miracles followed! Not occasionally. Always!

Well, almost always. There was this one time...

In Mark 6 we read about Jesus taking His disciples with Him back to His hometown of Nazareth. And Jesus did what Jesus does! He started to preach.

"Oh, I know. Many were healed, and demons were cast out, right? That's what always happens when Jesus shows up."

But that's not what happened at all. This time, it looked very different.

> Then they scoffed, "He's just a carpenter, the son of Mary and the brother of James, Joseph, Judas, and Simon. And his sisters live right here among us." They were deeply offended and refused to believe in him.
>
> —Mark 6:3

> And because of their unbelief, he couldn't do any miracles among them except to place his hands on a few sick people and heal them. And he was amazed at their unbelief.
>
> —Mark 6:5–6

Wow.

There is so much to unpack in these few short verses, but I want to start with this: They *refused* to believe in Him. You see, this verse just told us Jesus *couldn't* do many miracles. It didn't say He didn't want to. He couldn't!

Why?

Our belief is a *choice*—but not just a onetime choice. It's an all-day, everyday kind of choice. We like to choose what we believe based on what we can see and feel. The people in this story refused to believe. They made a choice. But why? Because of what they saw. Because of what they felt. Because of what they thought.

Remember?

This was Jesus' hometown! He rode His bike on these streets. He ate cookies at Mrs. Salome's house and played hide-and-seek in Shimon's orchard. "We know this guy!" would have been the dominant consensus. They didn't believe what Jesus was saying because they *thought* this was just the kid who… Do I even need to keep going? It doesn't matter how we finish the sentence because the words *they thought* make it a moot point!

None of this is about what we think.

In chapter 2 I told you that what you believe *about* God will determine what you receive *from* God. That is the reason Jesus couldn't do many miracles! They weren't open to receive them. He wanted to, but they wouldn't let Him. Not because they didn't want the miracles. Of course they wanted *that*! What they didn't want was to let go of themselves.

Let's break this down logically. Do you feel the same all day, every day? No. Of course not. Our feelings about people, places, situations, ourselves, and even God are constantly changing. Do you see or experience the same things every day? Again, no. The same reasoning applies.

Oh, and what does that mean? It means our belief can't be based on something that changes day by day or minute by minute. It must be based on something solid that never changes!

But there is another line we need to take note of in the story as well: "And he was amazed at their unbelief." Does that sentence make your heart skip a beat? It does mine! I mean, come on—Jesus is God in the flesh. Nothing catches Him off guard. So for the Bible to say that Jesus was amazed, that's truly saying something!

And did you know the Bible tells us Jesus was amazed not only this one time but two?

The second time we see Jesus was amazed is in Luke 7. But this story is very different. Here, we have a Roman officer coming to Jesus to ask Him to heal one of his servants.

Well, not exactly. The Roman officer didn't actually go anywhere. Instead, he sent some of his friends to talk to Jesus.

Now, at first glance you might start to think, "Well, that makes sense. He's a Roman officer. It would be out of line for him to go to Jesus himself. He might lose his job! What would his friends think?" Something along those lines.

It can be difficult to shift our mindset from what we think to what God thinks, can't it? If we don't ever stop to check *whose* thoughts we are listening to—ours, God's, or the enemy's—we can start to get off course without even noticing. And that is exactly what the enemy wants.

But is that really the reason the Roman officer didn't go to Jesus himself?

> So Jesus went with them. But just before they arrived at the house, the officer sent some friends to say, "Lord, don't trouble yourself by coming to my home, for I am not worthy of such an honor. I am not even worthy to come and meet you. Just say the word from where you are, and my servant will be healed."
>
> —Luke 7:6–7

Don't miss the *why* here! The officer sent his friends to Jesus not because he was afraid of anything! He sent his friends because of what he believed about Jesus.

Remember what we discovered in chapter 1: "*What* you believe about God is consistently affecting every—literally, *every*—single area of your life: your relationships, your finances, your family, your joy, your peace. Your *everything* is being affected—positively or negatively. It all hinges on what *you believe* about *who* God is and what *His* purpose is for *you*!"

Here it is, happening in real time!

This Roman officer was a man of authority. He had men who worked under him. If he said it, they did it, no questions asked. The Roman officer recognized the same power and authority in Jesus, but on a much larger scale!

He knew. He knew if Jesus just said the word, his servant would be healed! He didn't need to see Jesus. He didn't need to feel His presence. All he needed to know was that Jesus had said it was done.

> When Jesus heard this, he was amazed. Turning to the crowd that was following him, he said, "I tell you, I haven't seen faith like this in all Israel!"
>
> —Luke 7:9

Again, Jesus was *amazed*. Two times now we've seen this happening. Both times regarding belief. Faith. What was the difference? The aim.

The people of Nazareth aimed their belief about what Jesus could do at themselves. "We don't think You can, Jesus. That's what we believe!" They didn't say those words exactly. But they didn't have to. Your actions will shout your true belief louder than your words ever could.

The Roman officer, on the other hand, aimed his belief about what Jesus could do at Jesus! The same thing amazed Jesus both times. Trust. Faith. Belief.

So what about you? What about *you* amazes Jesus? Your faith? Your belief in His Word? How much you trust Him? Or your excuses? Your doubt? Your stubbornness to step outside the walls of "I thought"?

Don't let what amazes Jesus about your life be determined by what you see and feel today. Some days, it's going to be easy to choose faith. Other days, it won't. But neither should matter. Because we have a greater truth!

I told you at the beginning of this chapter that our belief can't be based on something that changes day by day or minute by minute—it must be based on something solid that never changes. Well, here it is! "Jesus Christ is the same yesterday, today, and forever" (Heb. 13:8).

The people of Nazareth missed out on some amazing miracles because they refused to believe. The Roman officer got his miracle because he trusted Jesus' word without needing to see a thing. One response shut heaven down. The other made heaven move.

Hebrews 11:6 says, "It is impossible to please God without faith." Did you catch that? It doesn't say it would be *difficult* to please God without faith; it says it is *impossible*. Your belief either invites God's power into your life or slams the door shut, leaving Him out in the cold. There is literally no middle ground.

Listen up, my friend, and lock this down. We have *got* to stop treating belief like a background thought. Stop filtering God through your feelings.

It's time to flip it—filter your feelings through God's truth. Let your faith be the kind that stuns heaven and shocks hell!

Let Jesus look at your life and say, "Now *that* amazes Me."

To access more content from Kelly K, scan the QR code or visit KellyKBooks.com/believer/ch7.

MARIA BUCHANAN

My testimony is a long one, so here's a short version: I had a traumatic childhood, raised two special-needs boys, and buried a third. I got divorced from an abusive husband and developed a rare neurological condition after an accident that cost me a finger. Was bedridden for two years and sick for sixteen years.

I ask God to convict me. Within months my life flipped upside down. God also started healing me in this time period. We moved from Alabama to Ohio. I started listening to Kelly about a year ago; then my husband started listening to him with me. Then we started listening to Ryan. Praise God for the positive changes we've seen in all areas of our lives. It's like learning at light speed.

We now have an amazing home church. I can see God working on everyone in our family. I can't get enough of the Word. I never want to disconnect from God again. Joe and I have been called to start a ministry to help people break generational curses.

Before I started to listen to Kelly, I thought I was better than the people I had come from. Kelly looks like the people I come from. I can see now that it's OK to be me—the way God made me to be—so that I can do His work. It's so freeing not to try to look like the person I think I'm expected to be. It's so freeing not to judge but to love everyone equally. I have so much to learn and so far still to go, but I'm super excited to see what God has in store for me.

PART II

MOVING FROM BEGGAR TO BELIEVER

CHAPTER 8

INSIGHT > EYESIGHT

Catalyst (noun)

: an agent that provokes or speeds significant change or action

: a person or thing that precipitates an event[1]

DO YOU FEEL it? The shift in your thinking? I hope so! However, if you feel like maybe you missed something because you don't notice anything changing yet—that's OK! God works in each of us at the speed we need, not the speed we want. And He definitely has no concern about keeping pace with others. Don't forget, roots have to grow down under the surface before anything starts to show on top.

Whatever the case may be, you are right where you belong.

Now, up to this point we have been focused on the why behind our belief (our faith). But now we're going to shift gears. Let's start to look at *how* to use this faith, as it was designed to be used.

What I am about to show you is the catalyst that got me where I am today. I used to live a beaten-down, broke, and busted life. I was *always* in need. I *never* had enough. I struggled just to get by. And the whole time, I knew the promises I read about in the Bible were real, but I never saw them in my life. I loved God, but I was always confused because my life didn't seem to look the way His Word said it could. You know—abundant, overflowing, more than enough, blessed, prospering in every season. Oh, how I wanted that life *so bad*. But it was always just out of reach.

Until it wasn't. Until God showed me a new way to think. A *better* way. And now I get to share all of it with you!

Are you feeling it? That feeling right before Christmas morning—the quiet buzz in your chest when you *know* something amazing is coming? This is exciting stuff!

In Mark 10:46–52 we find the story of blind Bartimaeus. Seven verses. That's all it took to tell his story. Yet we would need to write volumes of books to unpack everything inside it!

Over the next few chapters, I want us to examine his story. Not just glance at it—completely dissect it! This story is the heart of this book. When God showed me what I am about to show you, things changed. Not just for me spiritually but in every way possible.

So here is what I want to do. I want to ask you three questions. These three questions will be fundamental. No, not for this book. For your life. While we *will* use the story of blind Bartimaeus to answer them, you need to answer them in your life as well. Not just once. Monthly. Weekly. Daily. Hour by hour. Minute by minute and second by second. We all need to be asking ourselves these three questions constantly!

Because the truth of the matter is this: You're answering them already. You just don't know the questions. But your life is already answering them. With every action you take, every word you speak, every encounter you have, you are telling yourself and everyone else around you what you believe about these three questions.

"Kelly! Do we look like fish to you? Stop reeling us in! What are the questions?"

I was trying to build suspense. So without further ado, here are the three questions that will—strike that—*could* change your life forever. If you use them.

1. Am I a beggar or a believer?

This question, when taken to heart, will destroy the lie of the enemy every single time. It shines light on the truth and makes it extremely obvious if there are areas in our lives where we have believed a lie.

2. Who do you say I am?

This question forces us to see not only what we truly believe about God but also what He believes about us! It should go without saying that this question is *key* in our daily walk with God.

3. Who needs to be healed?

This question is bigger than you think. Pause for a second. Don't just glance past it. This isn't a throwaway question—it's a mirror. Because sometimes healing isn't just physical. It's not just about sickness, disease, or broken bones. Sometimes it's bitterness. Unforgiveness. Shame. A past you won't talk about. A future you're afraid to believe in.

"Who needs to be healed?" might be the most dangerous question you'll ever ask—because it doesn't just point to others. It points to you.

And each of these three questions—every single one—is meant to do the same thing: to *shift your focus* from what you see to what you know. These questions, unbeknownst to you right now, are going to be your catalyst for finding the life with God you have been looking for.

Let me explain it like this: When I was a little boy, maybe around five or six, my dad started playing this game with me anytime we were in the car. Well, he called it a "game." I thought it was torture!

It worked like this. We would be driving down the road, talking or listening to music, and out of *nowhere* my dad would reach over to the passenger seat and cover my entire face with his hand so that I couldn't see a thing. And if that weren't bad enough, he would then start describing to me things he was "seeing" out of the window!

"Oh, *wow*! Kelly! There's an elephant, right there on the side of the road. Oh, how cool. It's waving at us with its trunk! This is amazing."

Can you even imagine the excitement that comes from believing mixed with the utter frustration of not being able to see? I would pull at my dad's hand with all my might, *begging* him to let me see what he could see. But every time, every single time, right before he would take his hand off my eyes, he would say, "Aw, it's gone! You missed it!" And every time my dad would play this "game" with me, the things *he* could see just kept getting bigger and better. It went from an elephant waving its trunk to a dragon flying around our car while blowing fire and doing backflips!

I did *not* like this game. But then something happened.

I can't remember how many times we played. I can't remember how old I was the day it changed. But I can remember how it felt. One day, he put his hand on my face and started to describe whatever amazing, incredible, unbelievable creature he was seeing this time—and it clicked. It's not real!

With that very moment, God taught me a lesson that I would use for the rest of my life. Insight is greater than eyesight!

I reached the point in my life when what I knew to be true was greater than what I could see with my eyes. It didn't matter anymore what my dad said because I had the *truth* inside me.

Listen, my friend—when you know that you know that you know, it won't matter what you see, feel, or hear. And when it comes to living a life of faith and trusting God, this is exactly what it takes!

That is the point of our three questions. That's the entire point of this book: to get you to that place. Where you know that you know that you know, where you say, "What I believe about God—my *faith* in Him and His Word, who *He* says I am—trumps everything else."

This is the turning point, the moment when faith stops being something you talk about and starts becoming something you walk in, when the promises of God stop sounding like distant hope and start looking like your reality. This is when everything shifts from information to transformation. From surviving to living. From begging to believing. When you turn this page, think of it like a spiritual light switch—one that opens your eyes and shines light on God's truth and leaves everything else in the dark.

Jesus asked blind Bartimaeus, "What do you want me to do for you?" Bartimaeus replied, "I want to *see*!" (Mark 10:51). And now I will leave you with a question. A very important question. Before we flip that switch, I *have* to ask:

Do you want to see?

To access more content from Kelly K, scan the QR code or visit KellyKBooks.com/believer/ch8.

MARITA VENTER

This will probably be the longest and weirdest beggar-to-believer testimony.

My whole life I've lived close to God. I experienced His goodness and countless miracles, but my life was still falling apart. I can truly testify I'm one of God's most wayward children ever. He just never gave up chasing after me. (For example, when I turned eighteen, I "borrowed" my mom's car and drove to the next town with a casino to play poker and collect enough winnings to buy a horse.)

The hardest year of my life was 2024. Everything was falling apart: my health, my relationship, my financial stability, my mental health. I could not understand this. I was a devoted Christian. I went to church every Sunday, lived according to the Bible as much as I could, and prayed and worshipped as often as I could. I was teaching Sunday school. I begged God day and night to change my life, to reach down and just fix things, because I knew He could.

Days turned into weeks and months, but He didn't. So like humans always tend to do when desperate, I tried bribing God. I promised Him I would pray more on my knees, give up certain habits, and double down on all Christian activities. As you know, this doesn't work.

So 2024 turned into 2025, and, man, was I miserable, alone, and heartbroken. I'd been begging so much that I could not walk properly. I guess at age forty your back and knees will remind you that living on your knees isn't living at all.

So in January 2025 a miracle happened. There were two kids I taught when they were eleven years old who used to be atheists. They were now twenty-four and married with a beautiful baby. They came to my house and invited me to church. They had given their lives to God, and because they knew I loved them and prayed for them each day, they proudly wanted to show me their church and how it changed them.

There was only one problem: Things at my home were still toxic. When I asked to go to their church, I was met with scorn, dismissal, and almost hate. I decided to go anyway. It wasn't like the church we went to. People were friendly, welcoming, and filled with joy. You could feel God's presence—not in the flashy worship or the extras, like free coffee, but in the acceptance and love the people showed.

So with my sore back and bruised knees I sat in church just talking to God, begging once again. This time was different, though. It was like God was talking back. I would be asking why things hadn't changed, and the pastor would say, "God's time isn't our time." I would start complaining in my head about why all these bad things were happening, and the pastor would say, "Sometimes we go through things in our lives to change us, to make us desperate for God." I know God was answering my questions; I could feel it in my soul. I just didn't like the answers.

The pastor called for people who hadn't yet given their lives to Him to step forward. I felt this burning inside me, pulling me, but I argued with God. After all, I was a believer; I was even baptized. So I said, "God, if You want me to go forward, make me glow like a firefly or something because You know I don't do this kind of thing." I barely said it when the pastor turned toward our section. He said, "There is a lady here in this row with lower back pain who was awake this morning at three o'clock—God said He is waiting for you. He has an appointment with you." I went forward and surrendered my life to Christ. I was changed in a way that runs so deep that it almost affects your DNA.

When I got home, of course, I was locked out. In my attempt to climb over the fence, my shoe got caught. Hanging there, several feet in the air, face in a flower bed, I burst out laughing. Suddenly, it didn't matter anymore. It didn't matter that some people in my life didn't love me; it didn't matter that my health was worse or that I had no money, because all that mattered was that I found peace, acceptance, and love with God. There was no denying it anymore. I learned what it meant to not only give your heart to God but surrender your life to Him fully.

At that moment, I became a believer, not a beggar. I couldn't get enough of His Word. Before, I could argue biblical truths with the best of them, but it was just words—now the words came alive. I got excited with each new gospel song I discovered and listened to all the sermons I could. My prayers were answered not in the way I wanted but in a way I needed. My life hasn't changed that much physically, but that's OK, because what I needed wasn't a quick fix but to meet the Creator of the world and to realize His peace, love, and grace are enough. The realization that my life is His and He will provide in every need was all I ever needed.

CHAPTER 9

HAVE MERCY ON ME!

Mercy (noun)

: compassion or forgiveness shown toward someone whom it is within one's power to punish or harm[1]

: lenient or compassionate treatment

YOU FLIPPED THE switch. I'm proud of you! I don't think I need to spend any more time building excitement for what's to come. The fact that you are here right now speaks for itself. So let's jump right in.

Remember in chapter 1 when I presented you with this question? "What if we have based our entire lives on a belief that isn't actually true? Or maybe it *is* true, but it's not entirely accurate." Again, what would *partial truth* mean? This first question we need to start asking ourselves is what I had in mind: "Am I a beggar or a believer?"

And I told you something else we need to revisit as well: "What if all the devil has to do is alter what you believe—just enough? Just enough that it removes any power your prayers would have carried? I mean, that's the thing about being deceived. Someone who is totally and completely deceived will believe in their heart, 100 percent, that they aren't!"

So let's find out. Are we beggars or *believers*?

I know that sounds pretty straightforward. Like, you don't even have to think before answering. But we need to be honest with ourselves here. This won't work if we aren't. The truth is, no one wants to come right out and say, "Yeah, I'm a beggar. That's me!" However, if we really *are* beggars and we've been *deceived* into believing we aren't, we need to know!

First, what is a beggar? What does it mean to beg for something? In the most simple and basic terms, a beggar is someone who asks for what they need but who has no way of knowing whether they will actually get it. Just to be clear, I'm talking about being a beggar *spiritually*. This is about having a beggar mentality when it comes to God.

To a person with a beggar mentality, their entire life is an unknown. A mystery. One big question mark. They know what God's Word says, and they read the promises He gave them. However, instead of believing that those promises are theirs already, they beg for them, never knowing whether they will ever actually show up.

There is a major flaw in that mindset. Where is the faith? Where is the trust?

Instead, a beggar mentality is founded on wishing. "I *wish* I would get what I need. I *wish* God would make a way. I *wish*..." You get it.

A believer, on the other hand—that's a different story. What is a believer? In the most simple and basic terms, a believer is someone who is *fully* convinced. What are they fully convinced of? Anything! It doesn't matter. They just believe! And there is nothing you can say or do to convince them otherwise.

The best example I can think of to really drive home my point is conspiracy theorists. Oh, son! Have you met one? I'm not here to make fun or laugh—I'm actually impressed. Those people *believe*. Not only do *they* believe, but they want *you* to believe as well. And if you don't, watch out! You're about to get facts, evidence, testimonies, and Lord knows what else thrown at you. They are unshakable. Immovable. They are solid. Maybe *what* they believe is a little off at times, but the belief itself isn't. Honestly, if every

Christian on earth had the same faith as a conspiracy theorist, the whole world would be saved by now!

So which one are you? Which one was blind Bartimaeus?

That sounds like a ridiculous question, doesn't it? Especially regarding Bartimaeus. Let me start by giving you the story in its purest form—straight from the Bible.

> Then they reached Jericho, and as Jesus and his disciples left town, a large crowd followed him. A blind beggar named Bartimaeus (son of Timaeus) was sitting beside the road. When Bartimaeus heard that Jesus of Nazareth was nearby, he began to shout, "Jesus, Son of David, have mercy on me!" "Be quiet!" many of the people yelled at him. But he only shouted louder, "Son of David, have mercy on me!" When Jesus heard him, he stopped and said, "Tell him to come here." So they called the blind man. "Cheer up," they said. "Come on, he's calling you!" Bartimaeus threw aside his coat, jumped up, and came to Jesus. "What do you want me to do for you?" Jesus asked. "My Rabbi," the blind man said, "I want to see!" And Jesus said to him, "Go, for your faith has healed you." Instantly the man could see, and he followed Jesus down the road.
>
> —Mark 10:46–52

Chills. Literal chills! Every time I read or hear this story now, my spirit gets excited. And yours will too pretty soon.

The scripture says exactly what he is, right? "A blind *beggar* named Bartimaeus (son of Timaeus) was sitting beside the road" (v. 46). But don't forget, we aren't talking about being a beggar or believer in a superficial, physical way. We are talking about a spiritual beggar *mindset*. Does that apply to him? Let's find out.

> When Bartimaeus heard that Jesus of Nazareth was nearby, he began to shout, "Jesus, Son of David, have mercy on me!"
>
> —Mark 10:47

Now, that's interesting. Did you catch it? What was he "begging" for? Money? Food? Clothing? Shelter? *Any* of the things beggars generally ask for? Nope. He asks for mercy.

Before we unpack what that means, we need to take a time-out. I need you to understand that what you *do* for a living is *not* who you *are*. Yes, Bartimaeus was a beggar—by trade. That's how he made a living. But that's not who he *was*. For so many of us, our identity is based on what we *do* instead of what the Father says about us. We will dive deeper into that soon, but I needed you to at least start to see it now.

So why did Bartimaeus ask for mercy?

To understand the why, let's first look at the what. What is mercy? Simply, mercy is when you don't receive the punishment you do deserve. You did the crime but serve no time. That's mercy.

So why would a blind guy—a beggar who asks for what he needs to survive every single day—ask for mercy? I'll tell you why. Because of his belief. His faith—but not in himself. Not even in humanity. In Jesus. Do you really think that this was his request to everyone he encountered? I don't think that's the case at all.

I believe his request shifted from physical needs to a spiritual need because "Bartimaeus heard that Jesus of Nazareth was nearby" (v. 47). He knew he was about to have an encounter with Jesus, so his request changed!

Has yours?

Are you begging God for the same things you were trying to find in the world before you gave your life to Him? Are your prayers filled with requests for what you need to just survive, or have you figured it out already? I'm teasing what's to come, but I hope I've got you thinking.

For Bartimaeus to ask for mercy means something. It means he knew—he knew a few things, actually.

1. He knew he was a sinner and needed saving.

By asking Jesus for mercy, what he was really saying was, "Jesus, please don't give me the punishment I know I deserve!" When we see it like that, it hits a little different, doesn't it? But honestly, that's how it works for us all. No one comes to Jesus because their life is *amazing*. Why would they give that life up? We all come to Jesus initially for the exact same reason. We realize that we're a mess—a sinner in need of a Savior. Our lives are so beaten up and broken down, far from where we wanted to be, but there is nothing we can do to fix it. We are trapped in our sin and need someone greater than us to get out.

And that leads us to the second thing Bartimaeus's request shows us he knew.

2. Jesus is the answer!

He knew the only person in the entire world who could meet his request for mercy was Jesus. He knew that before he could ever ask for what he *didn't* deserve from Him (his sight), he needed to get past what he *did* deserve from Him (punishment for his sins).

What about you? What's the verdict? Beggar or believer?

Don't answer that—yet. There is actually a test you can take to find out exactly which one you are. Do you want to take the test? The results may shock or amaze you. Remember, a person who is deceived will believe 100 percent in their heart that they aren't. I'm not saying that *is* you, but could it be?

This is that moment. This is when the veil gets removed. This is when you start to see what you, yourself, *really* and truly believe about God. Don't let this moment scare you. This is a really good thing! How else can we get to the place of total trust and faith in our God if we have been believing a lie or a half-truth about who He is?

So what is the test? Simple. Let me hear you pray.

To access more content from Kelly K, scan the QR code or visit KellyKBooks.com/believer/ch9.

GINA LESLIE

My name is Gina. I wanted to send my testimony of what has changed in my life since I've been following Pastor Kelly every day in his Bible studies with us. He gave me the courage to change my words and thoughts and taught me how to pray with confidence and a thankful, repentant heart as I made my requests known.

It literally felt too good to be true as I started seeing my prayers come to life! I used to sound like, "Father, please, Lord..." "*If* You could..." "Will You please..." and so on. I sometimes found myself thinking, "I hope the Lord heard my prayer." Since Pastor Kelly taught me how important it is to pray with thankfulness above all, I can face anything without fear or doubt!

My daughter, a teacher, had been looking to change schools for *years*. She had been to interview after interview but had constantly been rejected. She was having her second-round interview for a school, and she desperately wanted to relocate there. She asked me to please pray for her. I told her I would. How many times do people say, "I'll pray for you," and you wonder whether they really do?

I began thanking the Lord for what I believed He could and would do. I pray the same way every day, with an abundance of thankfulness and repentance. As God is my witness, she called me Monday, shouting, "Thank you for praying, Momma! They offered me the position!"

I use this as an example—there are many more, but this one was so significant. She'd been interviewing for two years! I consider Kelly K Ministries my church, even though I'm far away. Learning from Pastor Kelly is such a blessing every day, in every way!

God cares for all of us with such passion, and He will with you too!

CHAPTER 10

THE CURRENCY OF HEAVEN

Currency (noun)

: something (such as coins, treasury notes, and banknotes) that is in circulation as a medium of exchange

: a common article for bartering

OK, LET'S REWIND just a bit. Blind Bartimaeus: beggar or believer? Remember that when he approached Jesus, he asked for mercy, not food. And asking for mercy is definitely evidence that Bartimaeus was a believer and not a beggar, but it doesn't quite get us all the way there.

But there is a verse, one verse that will remove any question at all. Do you know which one it is? The verse that *proves* Bartimaeus was a believer and not a beggar? The verse that stands out as the big faith moment? The one that proves, beyond the shadow of a doubt, that Bartimaeus was a believer and not a beggar?

Guess!

Did you say Mark 10:48?

> "Be quiet!" many of the people yelled at him. But he only shouted louder, "Son of David, have mercy on me!"
>
> —MARK 10:48

"Yep! That's my pick. That's the one. The people tried to shut him down, and he just shouted even louder. That's *big* faith right there!"

You know what? You aren't wrong. It took some massive faith to keep shouting for Jesus while the crowd told him to shut up. We've all been *there* before, haven't we? Believing with all our might only to have those close to us, and strangers as well, tell us how ridiculous our belief is. We will look at this part of the story a little later, but Mark 10:48 is not the verse I'm talking about.

You may be thinking, "Then it has *got* to be Mark 10:51."

> "What do you want me to do for you?" Jesus asked. "My Rabbi," the blind man said, "I want to see!"

"Come on, Kelly, that *has* to be it! He straight up asked Jesus to heal him. For you to ask means you believe you're going to get it. Right?"

Not necessarily. Remember, that's exactly what a beggar does. They ask for something while having no idea whether they will actually get it. That's not faith. That's wishing—a dice roll, at best.

Before I give you the big reveal, I have one more thing to show you: the why behind the why. *Why* it's so important that we find out *why* we believe what we believe. Remember, we receive from God what we believe about God. Take a look at this!

> And Jesus said to him, "Go, for your faith has healed you." Instantly the man could see, and he followed Jesus down the road.
>
> —Mark 10:52

Please tell me you caught that! When Bartimaeus finally got his healing, pay close attention to the words of Jesus: "Go, for I have just healed you"? Nope. "Go, for My Father in heaven healed you"? Nope. "Go, for because of all the good things you've done, you earned your healing"? Nope. Three swings, three misses. But you already knew the answer: "Go, for your *faith* has healed you."

Boom, son! There it is! What I have been trying to show you since page one! The belief *itself* is what healed him. In a very loose sense, he "bought" his healing with his faith. Because faith is the currency of heaven!

Listen to how absolutely absurd and absolutely true this next statement is: There is no amount of money that can buy a miracle from God. You just have to believe it already belongs to you. Oh, son, that gets me excited!

But please don't misunderstand me on this. When we receive *anything* from God, an exchange always has to be made. The good news is, your part in the exchange is very simple. You just have to exchange your faith and belief for His *already* finished work.

Let me show you what I mean. Look at these three verses, and you tell me what they all have in common. This will blow your mind!

> Jesus turned around, and when he saw her he said, "Daughter, be encouraged! *Your faith has made you well.*" And the woman was healed at that moment.
>
> —Matthew 9:22

> And Jesus said to the woman, "*Your faith has saved you*; go in peace."
>
> —Luke 7:50

> And Jesus said to the man, "Stand up and go. *Your faith has healed you.*"
>
> —Luke 17:19

Wow! Including the story of Bartimaeus, that makes four times Jesus said almost the exact same thing. Seven times throughout the Gospels in total, if you include the same stories from different accounts. If you have done much study on the meaning of numbers in the Bible, you already know what I'm getting at—seven is the number of *completion*. Double wow!

Now I'm not saying this is a little hidden gem God put in the Bible to show us that our faith is what completes the process of receiving His promises. I have no evidence to support that. But I can't say it's *not* either.

So what was the big faith moment for Bartimaeus? What did he *do* that showed Jesus he truly believed? Oh, you know, nothing much. He took off his coat.

"*And?* What else? That's *it*? That can't be it. I take off my coat all the time. Requires no faith at all. I mean, it may take some faith that I'll remember where I left it, but come on now, Kelly, tell us what it *really* is!"

That really is it. Mark 10:50 is our moment of *massive* faith: "Bartimaeus threw aside his coat, jumped up, and came to Jesus."

I'm going to be completely transparent with you right now. I have been teaching this story in churches, camps, and conferences for years. And my favorite part is when I get here: the big aha moment. I love to tell everyone how back in Bible times, if you were a beggar, you had to wear a special jacket, or "coat," that signified you were a beggar. A license to beg, if you will. I love this part because I can physically see the light bulbs clicking on in everyone's hearts and minds!

But is that actually true? Or just a preacher's fable?

When it came time to put it in this book, I needed to make absolutely sure that this was a fact and not just something we added to tug at heartstrings and generate an emotional altar call.

Zero. That's how many credible sources I found to back this statement up. I was heartbroken. I told God, "This completely destroys the book! This was one of the biggest points I needed to make: how Bartimaeus *knew* his begging days were over before he even received his healing. He came to You knowing he would *never* put that coat on again because *You* were the answer he was looking for. Now what am I going to do, God?"

Then a word popped into my mind, a word I hadn't heard or thought of since Bible college: *himation*.

The himation was a large piece of outerwear (like a coat or jacket) worn in those days to keep you warm. You know, perhaps while sitting beside the road. However, the himation would also have been an encumbrance when running. It's also worth mentioning that they weren't cheap. Most people would have only one. So the added detail of Bartimaeus throwing it aside, in the dirt no less, to run to Jesus for healing still demonstrates how great this man's faith was!

That's when it clicked in my heart. It doesn't matter! This is most definitely Bartimaeus's greatest moment of faith. That jacket coming off, whatever the reason may be, was the action that completed his faith.

There's an issue here. Which matters more—faith or action? In the eyes of the Lord, which is greater? My faith or my works? In James 2 we see this issue being addressed. James says something very interesting in verse 17.

Essentially, the people were arguing over what saves you—your faith in Jesus as the Son of God, or the good works you do for Him. Some said, "All you need to do is believe that Jesus paid the price for you to enter the kingdom of heaven. The work is already done!" Yet others protested, "What good is your faith if you can't see it in your actions?"

And that's when James dropped this bomb on all of us:

> So you see, faith by itself isn't enough. Unless it produces good deeds, it is dead and useless.
>
> —James 2:17

"Now, hold on there, James! My entire life I've been told, 'Just have faith,' 'You just need more faith,' and 'Faith is all you need!'

Now you tell me my faith isn't enough? Without doing works, my faith is *dead*? How rude!"

That sounds like a mean thing to say, doesn't it? To be completely honest, it sounds like something he would get canceled for saying in today's overly sensitive, ultrafragile culture. But why do we take offense so quickly? Why do we instantly shift the focus back to *us*?

And there it is. Without even noticing, our focus has shifted from Him to little ol' me.

In the next chapter, we're going to take a simple look at the why behind faith completing our actions. I'm eventually going to show you *exactly* why faith without works is dead. But before we do that, let me ask a question: What about you?

When it comes to running to Jesus for what you need, what does your faith *look* like? Not what does it *say* on social media or to others at church. I'm not asking about what you claim at all. I'm asking, What does your faith *do*? How could I see that Jesus is Lord of your life if you were unable to communicate through words?

Do you leave your coat on—just in case? Just in case Jesus fails, at least you have a life to go back to? Do you hold on to what the world says has value so that if this God thing doesn't pan out, you still have something? Do you keep that backup plan? That hidden credit card? That toxic relationship? Just in case Jesus doesn't come through?

Or do you have a "blind man running to Jesus while throwing your old life in the dirt because you're never going back and you're getting your breakthrough" kind of faith?

Don't answer yet. Just think.

We haven't gotten to the meat of this yet. But man, oh, man! The milk sure is good!

To talk about it with Kelly K, scan the QR code or visit KellyKBooks.com/believer/ch10.

JESSICA LEONARD

I started listening to Kelly a little over a year ago. I don't even remember which friend shared a video for it to be in my feed—maybe it was the Holy Spirit Himself. But I knew I belonged there. I'd never seen a pastor do a live broadcast, and I was simultaneously exhilarated and terrified. I listened and lurked in the background for the longest time.

You see, I had been feeling like God was trying to tell me things for a long time, but I had no idea how to listen or what to do with it. I spent most of 2023 surviving a double round of food poisoning—a peanut butter recall with salmonella and the frozen strawberries infected with hepatitis A. The Holy Spirit had pushed me to quit drinking right before this, and if I hadn't, I would not have survived.

God saved my life that year, because I went through all that without medical intervention or a support system. I spent months throwing up. I couldn't hold down food for more than an hour or so. It left me weak, with very little memory or will to live. I was yellow—even the whites of my eyes were yellow. For whatever reason the people I trusted in my life didn't believe me or didn't care. I should not have survived.

I remember lying in a lounge chair in the front yard and telling God, "I'm sorry I'm a mess, but if this is Your will for me to die like this, take me now and help my kids." I couldn't take any more—I was a goner. The next thing I knew, I was waking up in that chair with a gasp to the sound of a hummingbird flying away. (For the record, it sounds like a thousand kittens purring.) I knew God had saved and healed me, but why me? And what now?

After that, the dreams started. I was living in sin with a boyfriend at the time, and I had the most intense dream about waking up whole and happy in a home I'd never seen. I hadn't felt happiness like that since childhood, or maybe never. By that evening I knew I had to leave my boyfriend (who was a compulsive liar and cheater). I moved out and

got a job. I also started writing again and really wanted to write a song but couldn't finish it. I can hear parts of it, and once I had a vision of a beautiful blonde lady singing it.

My ex killed himself a few months after I left, and I was in shock. I almost went back—I was in such a place of shock and grief. I wasn't in the Word enough to hold fast under spiritual attack.

That's when I started listening to Kelly. I found a private school for my autistic kids for the first time and got a job working for a dear friend as an assistant to an arborist. On the surface things seemed to be getting better. Unfortunately, I kept ignoring small nudges to share Jesus, and I also hadn't tithed since childhood. I have two special-needs kids, one of whom, at eleven years old, kicked a toddler at the grocery store. Because of that, there really isn't a place for us in a brick church, and the hurt that goes with that runs deep.

I was drowning in guilt and shame. To drown out the bitterness, I smoked tons of pot. I had no clue how to get out of the falling-down rental we lived in. All I knew to do was listen to my church videos. Then there was Kelly. His live stream became a place of refuge, and it was having an effect.

I had been searching for a camper that would work for my kids, thinking that if we lived in a camper, it would make relocating easier on my special-needs kids. But I didn't know how to get one, so I did what Pastor Kelly said: "Father, thank You for making a way for us to get a camper. Thank You for knowing where we should go. Thank You for making a way out of no way." Little did I know, Hurricane Milton was His answer.

A tree fell on that old rental, and we now live in a 2025 Forest River Campsite Reserve 20JW in the driveway. I barely blinked. "Father, thank You for the storm." I've been cooking on a fire, using a generator, and washing with gallons of bottled water. The camper turned out to be a brand-new lemon. The landlord of the rental closed my utilities accounts and issued multiple code violations, so the city regards me as a squatter. I am battling rodents and thieves and spiritual attacks, and all I can do is say, "Thank You, Father."

I parted with my old boss, the arborist, on bad terms due to the stress of this whole situation. Despite that, he called me up and told me he was buying land and we could go there. God is working. I have no idea how I'm going to get this camper moved to the new property, or even what's next, but I know that He is a good Father and it can only get better from here.

For so many years, He guided me to work on my credit. Without that I could never have financed this camper. I'm not even surprised. I even watched an online service and saw the beautiful blonde lady who was singing my song in my earlier vision. I heard, "There she is." It might sound crazy, and it hasn't happened yet, but I know that I trust God. I don't have the ending yet, but there is so much more.

As things are getting really tight now, I've committed to tithing again, despite being on Social Security income. And I'm praying for others more than ever because I know He can use that too. If I help one person, it's worth it to me. Sharing really is caring.

I gave up cigarettes and finally quit smoking pot after thirty-one years. I can't wait to see what God does with that. I might look crazy, walking around saying, "Thank You, Father; I can do all things," and reciting every verse that comes to my mind—but I know He is here with us. My semiverbal son will sometimes spontaneously say, "Amen! Amen! Amen!" out of nowhere.

I'm not even worried. Thank you, Kelly and family, for listening to the call and teaching us to do the same through your actions every day. Some of us really do take a while to get it through our thick heads. Thank you for sharing your love of the Father and doing what you do. Amen.

CHAPTER 11

THE EXCHANGE

Exchange (noun)

: the act of giving or taking one thing in return for another

: the act or process of substituting one thing for another

Exchange (verb)

: to part with, give, or transfer in consideration of something received as an equivalent

: to have replaced by other merchandise

LET ME OPEN this chapter by saying I was *not* insulting you! I mean, that is what you were thinking, right? You caught it right away! When I said we haven't gotten to the "meat" but the "milk" is good, you *knew* I was referencing Hebrews 5.

> You have been believers so long now that you ought to be teaching others. Instead, you need someone to teach you again the basic things about God's word. You are like babies who need milk and cannot eat solid food. For someone who lives on milk is still an infant and doesn't know how to do what is right. Solid food is for those who are mature, who through training have the skill to recognize the difference between right and wrong.
>
> —HEBREWS 5:12–14

I wasn't insulting you at all. I was preparing you! What we are about to discuss is *not* chocolate milk with a twisty straw. This is a forty-eight-ounce tomahawk rib-eye!

If faith is the currency of heaven, let's say miracles, breakthroughs, blessings, and favor are the products of heaven.

So for example, when you go shopping at your local grocery store and you've finished making your selections, do you just walk out the door and go load up your car? No, of course not. You have to go make an *exchange* first.

The first exchange you have to make is your work for your wage—a paycheck. We work because we desire *products*! Food, clothes, shelter, entertainment, and so on. This is the *original* exchange.

Then you exchange your currency for a product. You take that currency you now have and use it to pay. There is always an *action* involved. You hand the cashier the money, you slide a credit card, you tap your phone. This action, or exchange, *completes* the transaction. It makes it official. Now you won't be tackled by a seventy-eight-year-old grandma at the door for not having a receipt! The exchange, or payment, is the action that completes your transaction with the store.

Now, let's take this logic to Scripture and make sure it fits.

> Jesus turned around, and when he saw her he said, "Daughter, be encouraged! *Your faith has made you well.*" And the woman was healed at that moment.
>
> —Matthew 9:22

A woman had been in need of healing (the product) for twelve years. But she had the currency—faith! She believed that if she could just touch Jesus' robe, she would be healed (the payment/exchange). And she was healed! That's the receipt—the *evidence* that the transaction had taken place.

> And Jesus said to the woman, "*Your faith has saved you*; go in peace."
>
> —LUKE 7:50

Another woman was filled with shame and guilt for all the past mistakes in her life. She knew she was a sinner and needed to be saved (the product). But she had faith—the currency! She believed Jesus was the only One who could save her from her sin, so she honored Him by anointing His feet with expensive perfume (the payment/exchange). And Jesus said her faith had *saved* her—the receipt, or *evidence*, that the transaction had taken place.

> And Jesus said to the man, "Stand up and go. *Your faith has healed you.*"
>
> —LUKE 17:19

There was a group of ten men who had leprosy and needed to be healed (the product). But they had faith—the currency! So they came to Jesus, and Jesus told them to go and show themselves to the priest (the payment/exchange). One man came back to Jesus afterward to thank Him for his healing—and he was healed! He got the receipt, or *evidence*, that the transaction had taken place.

> And Jesus said to him, "Go, for your faith has healed you." Instantly the man could see, and he followed Jesus down the road.
>
> —MARK 10:52

Bartimaeus had been blind since birth. He needed to see (the product). But he had faith—the currency! When Jesus called to him, he threw his coat on the ground before Jesus and even asked for what he needed (the payment/exchange). Transaction *complete*! And he too was healed—the receipt, or *evidence*, that the transaction had taken place.

Are you done chewing? Then let's take another bite!

> For the wages of sin is death, but the free gift of God is eternal life through Christ Jesus our Lord.
>
> —Romans 6:23

Let's dissect this verse completely so that we know exactly what we are dealing with here: "For the wages [payment/original exchange] of sin [work] is death [product]." And we also know that sin separates us from God (Isa. 59:2).

"Wait, wait, wait, Kelly—I see that there is work here, and I see there is a product here. But where is the currency? What even *is* the currency? How can *death* be the product if it is also the *wage*?"

Now we are getting somewhere! Let's look at the second half: "But the *free gift* [no work or payment required] of God is eternal life [product] through [exchange] Christ Jesus our Lord [His *finished* work]."

Oh, son! Are you catching this? Let's put it all together now!

"For the wages [payment] of sin [work] is death [product], but the *free gift* [no work or payment required] of God is eternal life [product] through [exchange] Christ Jesus our Lord [His *finished* work.]"

Now I can answer your question. What is the currency? If faith is the currency of heaven, think of fear as the currency of this earth.

You might think these are opposites. But in reality, they aren't. In fact, they are more alike than you know. Think about it like this: *Fear* wants you to *believe* something that *hasn't* happened yet. And what does *faith* want from you? To *believe* something that *hasn't* happened yet! Fear and faith both want the same thing! The difference is what *you* choose to believe. Now, let's apply this and bring it all together.

When we are born with our sin nature, we crave the things of this world. Why? Because of fear! We fear we won't have enough fulfillment in our lives, so we turn to other sources besides God to bring purpose. Out of fear we turn to substances instead of God. Out of fear we turn to websites and relationships instead of God. We feel like we won't ever have enough, even though the Bible tells us *He* is our provider. So we choose fear over faith, and we exhaust ourselves trying to earn a living.

You see, James 4:17 tells us, "Remember, it is sin to know what you ought to do and then not do it." Sin (work) isn't just stealing or lying, or even addiction and murder. Sin is simply going to *any* source other than God for what you need.

Work can be a sin if it's above God in your life. Your marriage, your kids, your friends, your car, your social media—anything can be a sin if it's above God in your life. If you know what to do and don't do it, that's a sin! And what is it we *are* supposed to do? *Trust God* with *everything*.

Is this starting to come together in your mind?

We are born craving sin. So we use our worldly currency (fear) to go after things that God has already promised to give us if we just put our trust in Him. And now, since we are choosing *sin* instead of God, *that* is our work: rebellion, pride, greed, lust, hate, envy, and so forth. And your work will always bring a form of payment. In this case the wages for sin is death.

However, sin doesn't actually bring fulfillment *at all*. All the things we try to do to feel free are actually keeping us chained to an empty life. When we finally realize this, that's when we start looking for another option.

God!

We must all get to the point where we realize we *can't* do this life on our own, out of our own works. Our salvation in Christ (the product) is not based on *anything* you and I will *ever* be able to do. We have the *promise* of salvation (the product) because of what Jesus already *did* (the payment/exchange). Notice anything different about this one?

Let's see—there *is* a product. There *is* a payment. But the currency? The receipt? The evidence? The original exchange—my work for currency?

Exactly! When it comes to salvation, things are *very* different! This is why we call it a "free gift"! The payment has *already* been made. So your faith (currency) isn't *buying* salvation at all!

Think about it, friend! Jesus already made the exchange for you. His work on the cross is what *allows* us to even have faith (currency)!

When you stand before the Father one day, He won't ask you which payment method you intend to use for your stay. He just wants to see the receipt showing that it's *already* been paid! *That* is what your faith (currency) and works are accomplishing!

Please notice that I didn't say payment here, because it's not about *you* paying. It's about you making an exchange. Even if we had all the faith (currency) on earth, it still wouldn't be enough to "purchase" salvation. If we could, why would we need Jesus at all? If it were up to *me* and I could do it on my own, then Jesus accomplished absolutely *nothing.* He went through the most horrible pain and suffering anyone has ever gone through—because He had to! Because we *can't* purchase salvation for ourselves.

Not to mention, if we could, it wouldn't be a "free gift" at all!

To access more content from Kelly K, scan the QR code or visit KellyKBooks.com/believer/ch11.

MICHELLE RAINWATER

I have been watching Pastor Kelly for a year now, and I have personally seen a huge change in my life, just from waking up saying, "Thank You, Father," and forgiving because He's forgiven me.

Last October is when it finally dawned on me that I needed to let go of my past. I watched Kelly's video about the woman caught in adultery

and Jesus coming in and saving the day. That's my story, and that day hit hard for me. I finally found peace. God doesn't see me as I once was but as who I am now. I am in right standing with God, and I can do all things through Christ who strengthens me.

I was ready to give up on my marriage, but by changing my mindset, I have changed my heart posture. I know God loves marriage, and as long as I am fighting for mine, God's got my back, and He'll help me through it. I don't scream or slam doors anymore. I can calmly talk to my husband, and I know when I need to keep my mouth shut.

I now speak in authority because I know God wants healing, love, joy, and peace. I thank God for all He's done and for all He hasn't *yet* done because I know His timing, His ways, and His thoughts are bigger and way better than mine. I am standing in the gap for my husband, knowing my God is still working in him, giving him the desire and the ability to do what pleases Him. That's what I'm standing on. I also know that if there is anything in me that needs to change, God will reveal it and teach me to remove it so I can be a better person for those around me. Thank you, Pastor Kelly, for teaching our family how to grow closer to our awesome Father.

CHAPTER 12

THE "FREE GIFT" OF SALVATION

Through (preposition)
: by means of; by the agency of
: because of

"OK, OK, OK, Kelly. I have to ask. I see that you put 'free gift' of salvation in quotation marks there. Why? What are you implying with that, huh?"

The reason I put "free gift" in quotation marks is because our modern use of these words and the Bible's use of them are *not* the same! We use the term "free gift" like it means you get something for nothing. However, no cost doesn't necessarily mean nothing required.

Now, before you start to disagree, let me show you something else.

There *are* times in God's Word when we see Him giving something for nothing. For example, in Genesis, Adam and Eve didn't do anything to be created. How could they? They didn't do anything to get paradise in the Garden of Eden. And they never earned dominion over creation. God just *gave*—no exchange at all.

In Genesis 12, when God called Abram and promised to give him many descendants, He didn't ask Abram to do something first. God just straight up said, "I will bless you! I will make your name great!" The promise was unearned and given before any action.

In John 5 the lame man at the pool didn't even show faith. Jesus just healed him! And I could go on! *However*, with all that being said, our salvation still doesn't make this list. Why? Because it isn't *free* at all!

"Yes, it is, Kelly. Romans 6:23 says so!"

As we saw in the previous chapter, Romans 6:23 says, "For the wages of sin is death, but the free gift of God is eternal life through Christ Jesus our Lord." I know! I understand what you are saying. But don't forget—the Bible is a mosaic. You can't zoom in too close.

You'll miss the forest for the trees.

If we zoom in to Romans 6 so close that we lose sight of the entirety of God's Word, I would agree with you! But if we zoom out a bit, we quickly realize our understanding of this concept is flimsy at best.

Now, you may be reading this right now and already know what I am telling you, and it is not a new revelation at all. (For some it is.) However, trust me on this: We are heading somewhere, and if this foundation isn't laid, *we are in great danger of destruction*.

The *Merriam-Webster Dictionary* defines *free* as "not costing or charging anything." I got my iPhone for free...when I signed a contract to pay a monthly service fee. So was the phone actually *free*?

The New Living Translation gives a heading to Luke 14:25–33: "The Cost of Being a Disciple." Here, Jesus straight up tells us! To paraphrase, He said, "Before you raise your hand in church and repeat after the pastor to receive your 'free gift'—*count the cost*. No money will be traded. But a trade still has to take place! I will give you *My* right standing with the Father in exchange for *everything you've got*!"

Wow, *everything*? That doesn't sound like a "free gift" at all!

That's why I use the quotation marks.

So why do I keep calling it a free gift, even if it isn't? Because it is! Does your brain hurt yet? I feel you, friend. But don't take a Tylenol just yet—keep reading. It will all make sense shortly!

So how can a "free gift" cost you everything? Let's tear this thing wide open and find out!

Now, to set things up a bit, we know that Romans 5:12, Psalm 51:5, and Ephesians 2:3 all show us that we are born into sin. We didn't choose it, but because of Adam, sin did enter the earth. And now each of us inherit that same sin nature. Just like we all want to leave a financial inheritance to our children, we also unfortunately leave them a sin inheritance as well.

> When Adam sinned, sin entered the world. Adam's sin brought death, so death spread to everyone, for everyone sinned.
>
> —Romans 5:12

Rebellion, greed, pride, lust, and so on have been passed down to generation after generation. We call that our "flesh." Our flesh craves the things of this world. Our flesh wants, straight up, the *opposite* of God *because* our flesh is born into sin. All because of Adam and his first sin.

And remember, the wages (payment) of sin (work) is death (product), right? What this means is that since your birth you have had a nature that *craves* to work for a product that is designed to kill you and keep you separated from God.

It should come as no surprise that each person, family, and generation has sin issues that seem to be passed down like an inheritance. Maybe your great-great-grandfather was an alcoholic. And so was your grandpa. And so was your dad. And now, so are you. Is that just a coincidence? I don't think so.

You see, when we read about the "free gift" in Romans 6, there is another word we skim past that is actually incredibly vital!

> For the wages of sin is death, but the free gift of God is eternal life through Christ Jesus our Lord.
>
> —Romans 6:23

Do you know which one it is? (Hint: It's our definition for this chapter.) You got it—*through*! What *through* means is that you and I can't climb our way to God. We can't build a tower tall enough or do enough "good things" to cancel out the wages of sin.

Religion will try to sell you that lie: "Do this, don't do that, give here, serve there, and maybe God will let you in." But that's not salvation. That's just more work, more wages, more death.

The gospel says something radically different: You don't go *to* God on your own—you go *through* Jesus. Jesus Himself said in John 14:6:

> Jesus told him, "I am the way, the truth, and the life. No one can come to the Father except through me."

Did you catch it? *Through.* That's the only doorway. Not your effort. Not your track record. Not your resume. *Through* Christ.

Think about it like this: His work was the payment. Our faith is still currency, but it doesn't buy salvation—because we have it! And our "works" after that? They're just the receipt—the proof of purchase that says, "Yeah, I've been bought. I belong to Him." The receipt doesn't pay for the gift; it just shows the gift was received.

Your salvation? What Jesus bought and paid for? That's absolutely *free*!

Going *through* Jesus, on the other hand, that's going to cost you. Not just a little. It'll cost you everything. Because you can't carry your own life through the cross-shaped door we walk through. You drop everything, pick up the cross, and go *through* Jesus!

And oh, my friend! The life you find on the other side is *so much better* than the one you were living before!

Now, I want you to ask God to give you revelation for what I am about to show you. This is *my* revelation that I received from God. For you it will just be secondhand revelation—for now. For this to become a solid foundation in your life, the Holy Spirit has to show you. And I have all the faith in the world that He will!

Pause for a second, and think about the definitions I included for *exchange* at the beginning of the previous chapter:

Exchange (noun)

: the act of giving or taking one thing in return for another

: the act or process of substituting one thing for another

Exchange (verb)

: to part with, give, or transfer in consideration of something received as an equivalent

: to have replaced by other merchandise

The very first thing I hope you saw is that there are not only multiple definitions for *exchange* but also two parts of speech! The word *exchange* can be used as a noun *or* a verb. Here is what that means: Jesus *is* the exchange, and He's the One who *made* the exchange!

When we count the cost and give up our lives for Jesus, *He* is the exchange (noun). Jesus did the work on the cross. He made the trade: His right standing with God for our sin. Then He *allowed* us to exchange (verb) our lives for His!

So let's bring Romans 6:23 back one last time. "For the wages of sin is death, but the free gift of God is eternal life *through* Christ Jesus our Lord." The world pays you death. Jesus gives you life. The cost for that new life is covered. The only question left is—have you gone *through* Him yet?

Because at the end of the day, salvation is not about what you *do*. It's about who you go *through*. And when you go through Jesus, you don't just get a new paycheck; you get a brand-new life.

And death? Yeah, not for you. Now you get to live *eternally*!

To access more content from Kelly K, scan the QR code or visit KellyKBooks.com/believer/ch12.

FRAN HEDKE-BARD

In May 2024 I was scrolling through TikTok looking for funny pets, a comedian, anything to make me laugh. That's when I heard the unmistakable "Hey, Christian!" from this guy with piercings and tattoos. Chances were good that he could show me something I didn't know. I was raised Catholic. I knew all the things to do and say during Mass, but I didn't understand much at all. It had been quite a while since I had been to Mass—like a "thirty-three-year marriage and four kids" while. I was *hooked*!

In 2022 I decided to make a career change to health care. I know now it is truly my calling. I took the class to become a nurse aide, then after a few months took another class to become a certified medication aide. In January 2024 I started a new job. In May I noticed how much weight my husband had lost. This man never, and I mean never, got sick. Even when COVID came through the house, it couldn't get him. In June he got blood work, X-rays, the works. On July 11 a colonoscopy gave us the answer: rectal cancer, stage 4, with liver metastases taking up over 80 percent of both lobes. They said that without intervention, he had less than three months to live.

We started chemo in August. I know y'all can relate with the whirlwind. Now we are thirteen months and twenty-seven treatments later, thanking Jesus for stabilizing this disease. He is down to one chemo drug with minimal side effects and has gained back the weight that he lost. Life is good; thank You, Jesus!

I never begged, "If it be Your will," because I had already learned from Kelly to be a believer. "Thank You, Jesus, for healing my husband" comes out of my mouth every day. I can see that God was at work in our lives before I discovered Kelly. I also know that if I hadn't found Kelly, I would not have noticed God's work. I would have been stuck, not handling this well at all. I might have been mad at God and probably would have turned my back on Him even more than I had. Thank you, Kelly and team—you have made my life so much better. Amen, amen, amen!

CHAPTER 13

THE TEST

Faith (noun)

: great trust or confidence in something or someone[1]

: firm belief in something for which there is no proof

DON'T ACT SO surprised! You should have seen this test coming from a million miles away! Everything we have discussed in this book so far has been leading us to the truth behind what *you* believe about *who* God is. What better test could there be? The only way to find out exactly what we believe *about* Him is to dissect our conversations *with* Him!

I apologize for making you wait, but you should know by now there is always a reason. I wanted to let that idea resonate inside your heart. You know what I mean? The idea that your prayers, in and of themselves, are essentially a test from the Father every time you pray—testing what you believe, testing your faith. I wanted you to focus inward and examine your own prayers while anticipating what this test would reveal.

Obviously, I can't hear each of you pray. What we can do, however, is look at examples of prayers from both a beggar mindset and a believer mindset. This will show you which one most resembles your prayers.

There is something I want you to do for me first. Pretty please? Make a note—in this book, on your phone, wherever. Write today's date with the words "the day everything changed."

Take a breath. Clear the noise. You're not just reading anymore;

you're stepping into a moment that could change everything. Let's start by looking at a prayer from a beggar mindset. That would sound something like this:

> *Hey God, it's me again. I was just wondering, if You could, please help us with our rent this month? We need $1,500, or we are going to be in serious trouble. Also, if it be Your will, please heal my spouse's back. They are in a lot of pain every day; if You could heal them, that would be such a blessing! And Father, my kids are far from You. If You wouldn't mind, help them find some friends who will get them back in church. You are so good! I give You all the honor and praise. In Jesus' name, amen.*

Does that sound like a prayer *you* would pray? Does that prayer sound accurate? Does it feel powerful? Do you think that prayer shakes heaven and stirs the heart of the Father?

Now, before we place this prayer under the microscope for closer examination, let's look at a believer-mindset prayer. That would sound more like this:

> *Father, I come to You today with a* huge *need in my life. We are short $1,500 for our rent, but I trust You! We may not have seen this coming, but You did. I know You've gone before me and made a way. I thank You in advance for meeting this need because* You *are my provider! And Father, I thank You for* more *than enough so that I can be a blessing to others in need as well. Father, I lift up my spouse to You today. I know You love them more than I do. It breaks my heart to see them in so much pain, so I know it breaks Your heart too.*
>
> *Thank You for a complete and total healing in their back, even right now, in Jesus' name. And Father, I trust You. I thank You for this healing, however You want to*

> *do it, whenever You want it to happen. Because I know it was already bought and paid for on the cross! And I thank You for the promise You gave me regarding my kids. I stand on Your Word. They may be far from You today, but You promised me if I train up my children in Your ways, when they grow up, they will not depart from You. Father, I'm not worried about them at all—I trust You. All these things I pray in Jesus' name. Amen.*

Does *that* sound like a prayer *you* would pray? Do you see the difference? Do you feel the difference? *That* prayer sounds accurate! *That* prayer feels powerful! *That* prayer absolutely shakes heaven and stirs the heart of the Father!

But why? What made the latter prayer so powerful and the former so weak?

You got it! *Faith.*

In both prayers the aim was correct. Both prayers acknowledge that it's God who makes a way and meets our needs. However, one prayer is full of praise and thanksgiving that the needs are *already* met, while the other just *wishes* they would get met—eventually. The first prayer is outlined in hope but filled to the brim with fear. Doubt. Uncertainties. The second prayer is outlined in faith *and* filled to overflow with trust and God's own Word!

You caught it, didn't you? The believer-mindset prayer quoted Scripture, at a minimum, eight times? Just so there is no confusion, I'll show you.

> *Father, I come to You today with a* huge *need in my life. We are short $1,500 for our rent, but I trust You!*

> Don't worry about anything; instead, pray about everything. Tell God what you need, and thank him for all he has done.
>
> —PHILIPPIANS 4:6

Trust in the LORD with all your heart; do not depend on your own understanding. Seek his will in all you do, and he will show you which path to take.

—PROVERBS 3:5–6

We may not have seen this coming, but You did. I know You've gone before me and made a way. I thank You in advance for meeting this need, because You *are my provider!*

I will answer them before they even call to me. While they are still talking about their needs, I will go ahead and answer their prayers!

—ISAIAH 65:24

And Father, I thank You for more *than enough so that I can be a blessing to others in need as well.*

And God will generously provide all you need. Then you will always have everything you need and plenty left over to share with others.

—2 CORINTHIANS 9:8

Father, I lift up my spouse to You today. I know You love them more than I do. It breaks my heart to see them in so much pain, so I know it breaks Your heart too. Thank You for a complete and total healing in their back, even right now, in Jesus' name.

So humble yourselves under the mighty power of God, and at the right time he will lift you up in honor. Give all your worries and cares to God, for he cares about you.

—1 PETER 5:6–7

> He personally carried our sins in his body on the cross so that we can be dead to sin and live for what is right. By his wounds you are healed.
>
> —1 Peter 2:24

> *I thank You for the promise You gave me regarding my kids. I stand on Your Word! They may be far from You today, but You promised me if I train up my children in Your ways, when they grow up, they will not depart from You. Father, I'm not worried about them at all—I trust You.*

> Direct your children onto the right path, and when they are older, they will not leave it.
>
> —Proverbs 22:6

> So don't worry about tomorrow, for tomorrow will bring its own worries. Today's trouble is enough for today.
>
> —Matthew 6:34

How do you experience the promises of God for yourself? This is how you do it! You see what God says and does in Scripture, and you pray that back to Him with *faith* that He will do the same for you. He is the same yesterday, today, and forever—remember? "I am the Lord, and I do not change" (Mal. 3:6). We will dive deeper into this soon.

There is something else I need you to notice in these prayers: What was so different about the words each prayer used to present these requests?

The answer is the key that will unlock the most incredible power you have ever experienced in your prayer life. This will be the missing piece you have been looking for. I am going to show you *exactly* what stirs the heart of the Father and causes the doors of heaven to swing wide open in your life. I'm telling you this in advance for a couple of reasons.

You may know *how* to use the right words to pray correctly, but that doesn't automatically mean there will be power in your prayers. It *always* comes down to your heart more than your words. Remember, it's about the *why* and not the *what*! This will be the mental shift that you need for the rest of this book.

So now let's look at the specific wording that each prayer contains.

The beggar mindset is filled with the word *please* and others like it that communicate the same idea: "if it be Your will," "if You could," "if You wouldn't mind," and so on. Phrases like these are essentially saying, "I *wish* You would do these things in my life—I just have no idea if You will."

Again, I ask—where is the *faith* in that?

In Matthew 21:22, Jesus tells us, "You can pray for anything, and if you have faith, you will receive it." And just so that there is no confusion, the Bible even gives us God's own definition of faith: "Faith shows the reality of what we hope for; it is the evidence of things we cannot see" (Heb. 11:1).

And right there you have it! Faith isn't just *hope*; it's the *reality* of *what* you hope for! It is *evidence* of what we don't see. Yet! To really drive this point home, let me show you some synonyms. Synonyms for the word *reality* include inevitability, certainty, fact, actuality.[2] Synonyms for the word *evidence* are proof, confirmation, validation, verification.[3]

Those words should be painting a pretty vivid picture in your head right now. Faith isn't about wishing at all! It's about *knowing*. That's why the believer-mindset prayer was filled with the words *thank You*.

So here it is, my friend: the key to unlock the door. The missing piece that's kept you puzzled. The "magic" words that from this day forward will be the foundation of every prayer you pray: *Thank You!*

Remember when Jesus was about to raise Lazarus from the dead? That was a pretty big request, if you ask me. While it may not take much faith to pray for your child's skinned knee after a bicycle crash, faith to bring someone back to life after they have been dead for days—that's another story! Now I bet you have read this story a million times, but with this new understanding, let me show you something. See whether anything hits you a little differently when you read it now:

> Jesus responded, "Didn't I tell you that you would see God's glory if you believe?" So they rolled the stone aside. Then Jesus looked up to heaven and said, "Father, *thank you* for hearing me. You always hear me, but I said it out loud for the sake of all these people standing here, so that they will believe you sent me." Then Jesus shouted, "Lazarus, come out!" And the dead man came out, his hands and feet bound in graveclothes, his face wrapped in a headcloth. Jesus told them, "Unwrap him and let him go!"
>
> —John 11:40–44

Wow! Jesus understood the value of thanking the Father *before* the miracle shows up. He didn't have to do that. He did that for those watching so that they would believe. But He also did it for us so that once we received the Holy Spirit, we would know *how* to do the same.

Thank You. We are about to look at these two little words in detail, but we need to return to Bartimaeus before we do.

There is something I would like you to do. Even before your understanding is fully complete, start removing the words "please," "if You could," "if it be Your will," and anything like that from your prayers. Today. Don't wait another minute. Instead, replace those words and phrases with "Thank You." You may have no idea what is about to happen in your life because of this simple adjustment, but I do. And I am so pumped for what's coming!

Don't get hung up on the "if it be Your will" part. I know that may be causing some red flags to rise. For now just trust me. We will talk more about that in chapter 14. Don't get me wrong—if you're praying about something the Bible hasn't promised, seeking His will makes total sense. But when most people use "if it be Your will" in their prayers, it's because they have *no idea* what His will is. However, you don't have to wonder about that at all. The Bible tells us *exactly* what His will is. And guess what? When you pray His Word, you already *are* praying His will!

Remember that note I had you write at the beginning of this chapter? Do you see now why I asked you to do that? I hope so. And if you thought it wasn't that important, I hope you've changed your mind. Because this is it! The first day of the rest of your life! You have just been given a fundamental truth that the enemy has worked relentlessly and tirelessly to try to keep from you, a truth that so many believers will never come to fully understand. But not you. You got it! You now know one of the greatest secrets in all the universe!

To put it plainly and hammer the last nail into the coffin of our old prayer life: You don't have to beg God for *anything*. All you need to do is start thanking Him for what He's *already* done for you!

And what has He already done?

Oh yeah. Everything!

To access more content from Kelly K, scan the QR code or visit KellyKBooks.com/believer/ch13.

YVETTA PENNINGTON

First off, my son is an addict. For the past fifteen years, my daughters and I have tried everything to help him. Unfortunately, I had become a beggar instead of a believer—begging for him to come home, begging

for his safety, begging God, "if it would be His will," to take him on home quickly and stop the suffering.

November 3, 2023, was a day I'll never forget. My son was living in a motor home across the road from our house in an empty lot. Somehow, the camper caught fire. In a panic I ran to get him out, but the camper door was melted shut. My daughter came running and tried everything to open the door but couldn't. As my daughter ran to get her children back into the house and away from the fire, I continued trying to get inside the camper, believing my son was trapped inside.

Out of nowhere, a man pulled me away from the fire. As I struggled to get away from him, he said, "He's not in there." I remember screaming, "My son is in there—help me!" Again, holding me tighter, the man said, "He's not in there."

The fire trucks and law enforcement arrived, and I was still unable to move, screaming, "My son is in there." Then, with an overwhelming calmness, the man holding me back from the fire said a third time, "He's not in there." As the fire department was putting out the fire, the man just disappeared.

No one knew who I was talking about. The fire department and fire marshal did the investigation and confirmed that my son *was not* in the camper. EMS checked my daughter and me for any burns or injuries from trying to get inside—nothing. We were both fine.

I looked for the man who saved me. One of our neighbors caught it all on their home security camera, and they could see me standing alone screaming but *no man* holding me. *Jesus* Himself walks this earth. *Jesus* is the only reason my daughter and I didn't get hurt that day. *Jesus* is the only reason my prodigal child is still alive today. I don't understand the path, but I do know Jesus knows all, and I trust in Him.

CHAPTER 14

THE POWER OF THANK YOU

Thanksgiving (noun)
: a public acknowledgment or celebration of divine goodness
: a prayer expressing gratitude

OK, WE'RE GOING to dive back into our friend Bartimaeus's story in the next chapter, I promise! But first, you don't want to miss out on the most powerful weapon you have as a believer, do you? I didn't think so!

I think we are all on the same page now, with a solid understanding of why faith is the currency of heaven. Our faith is just saying, "God, I trust You! I won't look to anything else for what I need. And since I *know* Jesus paid for it all, my faith can lead me to only one thing."

Now what if? What if God gave each of us something so powerful that we could access His presence *instantly* anytime we wanted or needed it? What if I told you that's *exactly* what He did? He gave you one of the greatest weapons you will ever wield: two words that contain more power than you can even fathom! Are you ready for it?

Thank you!

These aren't just some cute words you say to be polite after receiving a gift. These two words contain the power to change you, your family, your friends, and everything else. The power in *thank you* is the reason you get to confidently say you are a *believer* and not a *beggar*!

Allow me to explain. When you see your relationship with God as just a ticket to heaven, you will feel like you still have to do all the work yourself while on this earth—work for provision, work for peace, work for joy, work for fulfillment. My friend, as you may already well know, that is exhausting!

But it completely changes the game when you understand that Jesus didn't die to give you a ticket to a place. He died to give you a relationship with a person: God. His Father! And we *know* God is in control of it all. Everything belongs to Him. What could I ever want or need that He can't provide? We don't have to beg God for what we need or want.

My kids don't have to beg me for food. I don't know about you, but my kids go through my kitchen like tornadoes! They eat what they want without fear of punishment or shame or guilt. They don't even ask me half the time! They simply say, "Thank you." Why? Because they have a revelation of who their father is. They know and understand that if Dad bought it and put it in the pantry, even though they themselves didn't pay for it or earn it, they can go get it and eat it anytime they want!

That's how our entire lives should work with God. When it comes to our heavenly Father, instead of saying, "Thank You," after we get what we need, we say it *before*. This is how we "go get" what we need. We call that *speaking in faith*. And if you've been following along closely, you already know: That's what trusting God looks like!

Trusting Him is really all you need to do. When you trust Him and His Word, you will follow and live by it! Because you know there is no better way. This understanding is what makes the words *thank You* so powerful. Our words on their own contain no power until we put faith behind them.

Before we jump back to blind Bartimaeus, let me show you

one more thing to tighten your grip on thanking God *before* you have or see what you need in your life. Psalm 100:1–5 says,

> Shout with joy to the LORD, all the earth! Worship the LORD with gladness. Come before him, singing with joy. Acknowledge that the LORD is God! He made us, and we are his. We are his people, the sheep of his pasture. Enter his gates with thanksgiving; go into his courts with praise. Give thanks to him and praise his name. For the LORD is good. His unfailing love continues forever, and his faithfulness continues to each generation.

Did you happen to catch it? One of the most powerful truths of all time is hidden right in the middle of this tiny psalm. Hidden right in plain sight!

"Enter his gates with thanksgiving."

Oh, son! There it is! This verse just told us that we *enter* His gates with *thanksgiving*. You know what that means, right? Anytime you use the words *thank You* fueled with faith, you enter into the presence of God!

Think about that for a minute. You don't need a temple. You don't need a priest. You don't even need a good day. You need only two words to enter His presence: *Thank You*.

Now check this out: Can fear stand in the presence of God? Nope. Can stress, anxiety, depression, shame, or guilt stand in the presence of God? Nope! Can lack, loss, or limitation stand in the presence of God? No way! Are you smiling yet? You should be—this is incredible!

Now let's pair our new revelation from Psalm 100 with Philippians 4:6–7, which says,

> Don't worry about anything; instead, pray about everything. Tell God what you need, and thank him for all he has done. Then you will experience God's peace, which

> exceeds anything we can understand. His peace will guard your hearts and minds as you live in Christ Jesus.

Now at first glance we may want to stop reading after the first thought. "Don't worry about *anything*? Yeah right, Paul. That's not even possible! And pray about *everything*? When do I have time for that?"

But wait. Let's start at the end and go backward: "Then you will experience God's peace, which exceeds anything we can understand. His peace will guard your hearts and minds as you live in Christ Jesus." Who doesn't want that? Am I right? Peace that exceeds our understanding. Peace that guards our hearts and our minds. Um, yes, please. Sign me up!

Now let's keep reading backward to see how we can make that happen in our lives: "Thank him for all he has done."

Light bulb!

You want perfect peace? Hmm, where could that be found? Oh! In the presence of God! If there was only some way we could enter His presence anytime we wanted. There is. "Thank You!" Again, those are the "magic" words to *literally* enter His presence whenever you want. And since stress, anxiety, worry, and fear can't stand there, you will always find peace.

But let's not stop there. It keeps getting better. What's the next line in reverse? "Tell God what you need." OK, we are getting somewhere now!

We are believers, not beggars. So we know we don't need anything except faith! Faith in the *finished* works of Jesus. And we know faith speaks before it sees. So if I see a need in my life, I don't have to beg God for it at all. What do we do instead? Exactly! Say thank You!

So when this verse says to "tell God what you need," we already know. That means start *thanking* Him *now* for what you believe He is going to do in this situation.

And that leads us straight to the next line. "Pray about

everything." That's what we are doing when we say thank You to God. We *are* praying. And if I am thanking God all day long, I'm praying about *everything*! That's how we pray continuously.

And for the last line, "Don't worry about anything," do I even need to tell you? How could you ever be worried if your entire day is filled with thanking God? You can't. You won't be! The impossible part of this is not "don't worry about anything." What's impossible is worrying while in the presence of God!

Are you getting excited yet? Are you just itching to go pray? I hope so!

This understanding right here is what led me to start seeing mountains move in my life. This revelation of the power of *thank You* is where I started to see chains break and heaven move. And I know you will soon say the same!

Do you see now why saying please is weak and saying thank You is so strong? Of course you do! So do *that*. Remove *please* from your prayers. *Thank You* implies the *please* was already there! Remove "if You could" and "if it be Your will." You need only two words to activate power in your prayers. Just say, "Thank You!"

And here is what makes this my go-to weapon in my spiritual tool belt. Even if you don't specifically know what to thank Him for in the moment, it doesn't matter. You can thank Him for anything! The breath in your lungs, the shoes on your feet, the wind on your face, *anything*. It all puts you in His presence. And I'm telling you—that's the only place you want to be!

Maybe you are reading this right now and thinking, "Kelly, my life is so bad, man. I truly don't have anything to thank Him for." If that's you—first, that's a lie of the devil. There is *always* something to be thankful for. And second, you aren't alone. Lots of people feel that way. Now let me show you how to fix it.

If you truly can't think of anything to thank God for, start by thanking Him for what He *didn't* do. Thank Him for that person you wanted to marry, but now you are so glad you dodged that bullet! Thank Him for the job you *thought* you wanted, only to find out you would have been *miserable* there. Thank Him for all the horrible things you went through that didn't break you. That didn't kill you. That actually only made you stronger. Because when you start to thank Him for what He *didn't* do, you're going to start to see what He *did* do all along! It's not that God wasn't working in your life; you simply didn't have your focus aimed right.

You thought He was silent, didn't you? You thought He was absent. But maybe the no was actually His mercy. Maybe what you thought was a closed door was Him protecting you from the room you weren't meant to walk into. Maybe His plan is, was, and always will be way better than yours. You just have to *trust* Him.

Now it's your turn.

Put this book down, and go say, "Thank You," to the Father! His presence is going to bring you to perfect peace. And if you're anything like me, that's exactly where you need to be right now!

To access more content from Kelly K, scan the QR code or visit KellyKBooks.com/believer/ch14.

SCOTT RAPER

You have talked about going from a beggar to a believer. I just want to say you have described my journey with God to a tee. For many years, I was living on secondhand Jesus. I believed in who He was and what He had done for me and who the Father was, but all I ever heard was a watered-down sermon: "Put your hand up, say a prayer, and you're good." I had a hole that I was filling with pornography, prescription drugs, and chasing things that were no benefit to the kingdom.

I have been a paramedic for thirty-plus years. I was accused of doing something I did not do. However, I did make comments that

were *way* out of line. They told me that if I surrendered my license to practice medicine, I could reapply in a year and come back to work again. I went to Cozumel, Mexico, to become a scuba diving instructor.

What a way to be put into the fire. Cozumel was full of bikini-clad women from all over the world. I was using adult websites and stepping outside my vows with my wife. Long story short, I spent close to a year there, seeing the beautiful art of God in the seas, the land, and the people. My favorite memory while diving was seeing a large fish that had its back fin bitten off by something bigger. That fish had faith that he was the biggest fish on the block, and he wasn't—but he came through it with the Lord by his side. Thank You, Father.

When I came home, I reapplied for my paramedic license and was denied. I was still being judged for what I had not done and what I had said. I was going deeper into depression. I was angry at God for putting a love for being a paramedic in my heart. I had been doing this for over thirty years, and I still did not listen to God.

I was flipping through Facebook, and I saw this guy who dressed like a rocker preaching the Word of God. I stayed for only a second, and then I went on to another reel. But God has a plan; He kept dropping the video in my reels. So I finally watched one about prayer—Kelly and his in-your-face truth. For years I was a beggar. God showed me the occasional glimpse of what could be if I was a believer. I took what Kelly was saying and applied it. I thanked God for everything that He had done for me and thanked Him for seeing me through this season of fire.

I told God, "I know that this will be done according to Your plan, not mine. I know that if this does not go the way I want, You have bigger and better plans for me." For several weeks I prayed that way two or three times a day. I was being blessed by people helping and guiding me into what I needed to do with my licensure—all God's plan. The day of my appeal came; I felt a peace come over me. I told the judge what I knew; I presented the several letters that had come from friends of mine. The agency presented their side. Needless to say, they lost. Their case was full of half-truths, assumptions, and judgments.

God put me where He wants me right now. I am back on an ambulance working with people who look up to me. I am doing my best every day to live like our Father. Today on a call, I mentioned to a firefighter I liked the cross on his radio holster. He told me he catches a lot of flak for it. I put my hand on his shoulder and told him, "I will never give you grief, and I will back you every time." I also told him my faith in God is what has saved me.

Every day, multiple times a day, I pray to the Father. Not prayers of begging or asking but powerful prayers of a believer, thanking Him for everything. Thanking Him for a memory of a fish swimming around with no top fin but owning the reef with his faith in our Father. The faith of a mustard seed will and does move mountains.

CHAPTER 15

WHO DO YOU SAY I AM?

Contrast (verb)

: compare or appraise in respect to differences

Contrast (noun)

: a person or thing that exhibits differences when compared with another

THERE IS NO question more important in your life than this: Who do *you* say Jesus is? Not who does your pastor say He is. Not who does your church say He is. Not even who the Bible says He is. Who do *you* say He is?

That question doesn't come with multiple-choice options. It comes with eternal consequences.

You remember the three questions we are asking ourselves using the story of blind Bartimaeus, right? The first is, "Am I a beggar or a believer?" And we definitely know how to test and answer that one now! And now that we've been learning how to speak in faith, how to pray with authority, how to say, "Thank You," before we see the breakthrough—let's talk about why any of that works.

It only works when you know the One you're talking to. And that all depends on your answer to this question: "Who do you say I am?"

Now, in Mark 10, when we are first introduced to blind Bartimaeus, we see him calling out to Jesus from the side of the road. But who does he say Jesus is? "When Bartimaeus heard that Jesus of Nazareth was nearby, he began to shout, 'Jesus, Son of

David, have mercy on me!'" (Mark 10:47). The Son of David? I thought Jesus was the son of Joseph!

Don't worry—we will get to "Son of David" very soon. But let me show you another critical piece of this puzzle as well.

If we go back two chapters to Mark 8, we find Jesus asking His disciples the very same question I'm presenting to you. And I don't think it is a coincidence that He asked them this question *before* they encountered Bartimaeus.

Sit tight. I'll explain. In Mark 8:27–29, we read,

> Jesus and his disciples left Galilee and went up to the villages near Caesarea Philippi. As they were walking along, he asked them, "Who do people say I am?" "Well," they replied, "some say John the Baptist, some say Elijah, and others say you are one of the other prophets." Then he asked them, "But who do you say I am?" Peter replied, "You are the Messiah."

Before we get too deep in the scripture, let's examine the question a bit first. "Who do you say I am?" Now, if I were to ask *you* that question in regard to *me*, we would get many different answers. You may say, "An author." Some might say, "A pastor or preacher." Some may even say, "A social media influencer."

But hold on—my wife will read this book too! She might say, "a husband" or "a father." Oh! And the rest of my family and friends will (hopefully) read this book as well. They might say I'm a brother, a cousin, a son, a dad, a nephew, or a best friend.

So who is right? Which answer is correct?

They all are! Every answer given above *is* an accurate description of who I, Kelly K, am. The difference in each of these responses is based on the relationship each individual *personally* has with me. Remember when I said my kids move through my kitchen eating food like tornadoes? I told you that they don't beg me—instead, they just say thank you. But what was the *why* I gave you?

Because they have a *revelation* of who their father is!

My kids know I will provide for them. They know they don't have to worry about food on their table, clothes on their bodies, or a roof over their heads. They have no worry about those things at all because of *who they say I am*.

Am I painting this picture clearly enough for you to figure it out on your own? Jesus first asked His disciples, "Who do *people* say I am?" Why did He ask that? Why does it matter who other people say Jesus is?

Because of the next question: "Then he asked them, 'But who do *you* say I am?'" Jesus was getting the disciples' hearts and minds ready for a contrast. He was drawing a line between public chatter and personal revelation.

He was saying, "I know you hear the talk around town about Me. It goes both ways. But those people only see Me at a distance. You see Me up close. You spend time with Me daily. The people's revelation of who I am and your revelation of who I am, at least at this point, *should* be radically different!"

And the same goes for me and you.

Your belief about and faith in God will always be determined by how close of a relationship you have with Him. Relationships aren't one-way streets. They have to go both ways.

If Jesus asked you personally, right now, "Who do *you* say I am?" would He say your answer came from intimacy or secondhand information? Is your view of Him built on relationship or rumor?

Because the *truth* is He gave us access to Himself and His presence anytime we want. If we choose *not* to spend time there, we have no one to blame but ourselves when our relationship with Him isn't where we know it needs to be—or even *want* it to be.

The question we need to ask now is, "What do we really want?" Jeremiah 29:13 out of *The Message* Bible says it like this:

> When you come looking for me, you'll find me. Yes, when you get serious about finding me and want it

> more than anything else, I'll make sure you won't be disappointed.

"You won't be disappointed"! Wow! I absolutely *love* that. But let's get real. You have been disappointed in your relationship with God, haven't you? It's OK to say yes. I have too. But I also wasn't really looking for Him then. He was more of a "get out of jail free" card to me back in those days. And when my begging and pleading for what I *thought* I wanted or needed didn't happen, I got disappointed. I cried out when I was in trouble, but when things are good, who needs God?

I've been there too, friend.

What I'm trying to get you to see is, if you ask yourself today, "Who do *I* say Jesus is? Who do *I* say the Father is?" and your truthful answer isn't an immediate, "He is my everything!" that's OK. Well—it's OK for today. But it will never be OK for *you* again. You know too much now. You understand what the answer to this question actually means for your life.

So yeah, you're OK. It's just evidence that you need a greater revelation of who your Father is!

The reason my kids don't worry about anything that they may need is because they spend so much time with me. They have seen me prove faithful time and time again in their lives. There is *no doubt* now—if Dad has it, I have access to it. If Dad bought it, I get it too. If Dad says it, his word is good! That kind of faith, trust, and certainty isn't just given or received. It's built. It's intentional. It's sought after. And when it comes to our relationship with God, while He doesn't need to build faith or trust in us, we absolutely have to build ours in Him. We do that by spending time in prayer and reading His Word. We listen to sermons, and we read books like this.

"Wait a minute there, Kelly. Now it sounds like we are *working* to have a relationship with God. Didn't Jesus die to give us the 'free gift' of access to God? Isn't that what *you* told us?"

Oh, friend! You are absolutely correct! We can't work for or earn our relationship with Him. The relationship is already yours. Jesus gave that to you, and you accepted it by giving up your life for His! I said we have to *build* the relationship we already have. Every healthy relationship should change and grow over time.

Here's a very tough pill to swallow: If your life today, and your relationship with God today, is the same as it was when you first came to know Him—something is *horribly* wrong.

I'll show you like this, and then we can move on, I promise!

When I saw Lindsay Davis DJ-ing at a Midland, Texas, club late in 2006, I instantly knew I wanted to be in a relationship with her. I knew I wanted her to be my wife, honestly! But she didn't know *me*. For this to go both ways, I had to put myself out there. I introduced myself. I started a friendship. I began to spend time with her, and wouldn't you know it? We went from acquaintances to friends, to dating, to engaged, to married. Lindsay Davis may have walked into that church on March 6, 2010, but Lindsay Kopp was the one who walked out. That's identity, not ceremony. That is the power of covenant!

You see, all relationships have to be built. They can't be bought. They can't be earned. It takes two people wanting the same thing: to grow together.

God put Himself out there by giving His Son's life so you could get to Him. He showed you how much a relationship with *you* is worth to *Him*. He even offered you a name change as well: *sinner* to *saint*.

But what is a relationship with *Him* worth to *you*?

Is it worth your time? Because that is what it takes to know Him more. Time. Time in His presence. Time reading His Word. It is the one thing more valuable than even money on this earth. The one thing you can spend but never earn more of is time.

I'll answer for you. A deeper relationship with the Father is *absolutely* worth all the time you have!

Now let's pause for just a second. Can I be real with you?

I don't want to hurt your feelings, but I believe this needs to be said. If you spend more time defending your theology than actually spending time with the God you claim to know, you might not actually know Him.

If your answer to "Who is Jesus?" is based on what you heard growing up instead of what you've seen Him do personally, you're living off someone else's testimony, someone else's time in His presence. I call that "secondhand Jesus." And the problem with secondhand Jesus is this: You can't fight hell with someone else's revelation. You need your own.

You see, that's not faith at all. That's fandom.

So I say let's fix it. And the fix is simple. Spend more time with Him!

Let me end this chapter with Jeremiah 29:13 out of *The Message* one last time. Read it, and let the words sink down into your heart, not just your mind. And truly grab hold of the last line:

> When you come looking for me, you'll find me. Yes, when you get serious about finding me and want it more than anything else, I'll make sure you won't be disappointed.

Let's look for Him together. Let's get serious about finding Him. Let's want our relationship with Him more than *anything* else. Let's build *that* relationship, friend. And trust me when I say, *you won't be disappointed.*

To access more content from Kelly K, scan the QR code or visit KellyKBooks.com/believer/ch15.

JAZMIN CRUZ

I started seeking God for truth in 2022, which led me to Kelly K Ministries in early 2023. As I grew my relationship with God by getting into His Word daily, God directed me toward Kelly for a better understanding of His Word.

Being Mexican and growing up in a Catholic home, I always knew there was a God, but I never had a relationship with Christ Himself, nor was I ever encouraged to. I reached a point in my life when according to "the world," I should have been beyond happy and satisfied. I was driving a new Benz each year, living in a million-dollar home with a millionaire boyfriend who bought me anything I asked for. But I still felt empty inside. I knew something was missing. I also knew it wasn't anything materialistic, so I had to dig deeper. That's when I started seeking God for truth and answers, and boy, did He show up.

Right around the time God led me to Kelly, I was diagnosed with a huge brain tumor. It was December 2022 when I walked into an ear, nose, and throat specialist thinking I needed a tube in my ear because I had water caught in there that would not drain. (All I could hear out of my right ear was a sound like water moving around.) I realized it was more than that when I suddenly had five doctors in my room, and they all looked confused. One said, "There is something growing on your eardrum, and we have no clue what it is. We need an MRI done right now. You can drive to the hospital, or the ambulance can take you."

So I drove and had it done. Turns out it was a huge brain tumor that had grown onto my eardrum, blocking my hearing and not allowing my ear to drain as it should. The doctor said they needed to do a biopsy through my nose to cut a piece off and study it. So we did that the following week, and I was told we would watch it for the next six to twelve months to see whether it was growing, shrinking, or changing in size at all.

For the next year (all of 2023), I watched, listened, and learned so very much from Kelly. This guy brought me closer to God than I had ever been, and the best part was I understood everything he was teaching me. I was super excited to get to know my Creator and so much more. When Kelly started teaching on being a believer, not a beggar, it all made sense to me.

With everything going on in my life at that time, I knew that this teaching was for me. I took it all in and completely changed the way

I prayed and talked to God. I replaced *please* with *thank You* when I prayed, and it changed my life. I honestly never really worried or thought about the brain tumor. I had a peace once I knew what it was. In 2023 everything in my life changed for the better. In obedience to God, I walked away from my relationship with that millionaire and never looked back.

In my journey of seeking God, I understood the power of words and the impact they have on our lives. I told my parents, my sister, my brother, and one friend about the tumor, and I told each one of them, "Do not tell anyone about it." They asked me why not, and I said, "If they're not going to pray to God and thank Him for my healing, they will only be giving it life by talking about it, and that's not what I want."

They understood—after all, I've always been the "crazy" one in my family. My mom did ask whether she could share with her Bible study group, and I said yes, of course. Other than that, I shared it only with Kelly for a few months.

I was scheduled for surgery in November 2023. I told Kelly it was OK to share with everyone on the live for prayer. My faith was already above anyone I know because of the things God had shown me, but once I started praying like a believer and saying *thank You* instead of *please*, it just gave me that extra little push I needed. I've never questioned God. Not once did I ask Him, "Why me?" when I was diagnosed. I understand who I am and who He is, and I have laid down my life.

After a thirteen-hour brain surgery, I woke up the next morning to my neurosurgeon saying, "The surgery was a success, but we will need a second surgery because I was able to remove all the tumor from the top right area, but I could not get to the back part. Since I had you under for thirteen hours, I couldn't keep you under much longer."

I was on lots of medication, but I clearly remember my response to him: "Don't worry; Jesus got it. No need for another surgery."

He looked at the doctor standing next to him and then at my mom and said, "She's feeling good; she won't remember this."

My mom looked at me, and I said, "Oh, I feel great, and I will always remember this. Just like you told me to not be scared when I woke up from surgery because my eyes would be swollen shut and bruised purple, blue, and black, and you see both my eyes are wide open and there is no bruising. That's because my God has the final say. I respect and appreciate you as my doctor, but I know who my Father is and that Jesus paid for it all two thousand years ago, including my healing."

By this time he had had enough of me and said, "OK, we will see in six months when you have the next MRI," and then he left the room. They also told me I would be in the ICU for five days and then be put into a regular room for three to five days. Every day, I said, "Thank You, Father, for my complete and total healing. You are perfect, and if I am Your creation, so am I. What an honor to be Your daughter. Thank You, Father." I made sure to say it out loud while in the hospital so the nurses could hear me.

I was there for three days, and they sent me home directly from the ICU. The nurses would stay in my room listening to me talk about how good our God is. They told me my room was refreshing to them because I was the only person in that hospital who did not complain. Instead, I looked for the positives in every situation, always giving God the glory.

In July 2024 I went in for my six-month MRI checkup. I thanked God in advance for the clear results. I said, "Thank You, Father, that You have gone before me and removed the tumor from my body." Kelly and the team did the same, as well as my Bible study group.

The day before the MRI, out of obedience I went up during altar call and allowed one guy to anoint me with oil and pray over me. He said, "We thank You, Father, that when they see the images from the MRI tomorrow, they will all be shocked and say, 'It is gone; there is nothing there. The tumor has disappeared.' And Jazmin will say, 'All glory to my Lord and Savior, Jesus Christ, who paid for it all, and by His stripes I am healed.'"

Needless to say, *that is exactly how it happened*. My neurosurgeon thought he had the wrong MRI results when he opened them and scrolled through them. He said, "It's gone."

I looked him in his eyes and said, "Do you remember I told you Jesus got it?"

He smiled and said, "Yes, you did."

I pray this helped grow his faith, as well as that of anyone else who reads my testimony. Thank you, Kelly, for teaching me how to pray with boldness, exactly as what I am: a creation of God. What an honor to know God chose me before I could choose Him.

CHAPTER 16

WHY DO WE KNOW HIS NAME?

Messiah (noun)

: the expected king and deliverer of the Jews

: a professed or accepted leader of some hope or cause

OH, SON! WE are in the thick of it now! Do you see *why* it is so very important that we have an answer every single day? An answer to one: "Am I a beggar or a believer?" And two: "Who do you say I am?"

These questions are absolutely imperative in our daily lives and walk with God. They keep us sharp, laser focused, and on point! These questions will keep your physical and spiritual eyes from wandering. From staring at the wind and the waves to the One who can walk on water. And we still have one more question to get to.

Before we can continue on to our third question, however, we need to complete our understanding of question number two. And to do that, we need to go back to blind Bartimaeus in Mark 10. Buckle up, buttercup—we're going for a ride!

Who did Bartimaeus say Jesus was? Let's look and see:

> When Bartimaeus heard that Jesus of Nazareth was nearby, he began to shout, "Jesus, Son of David, have mercy on me!" "Be quiet!" many of the people yelled at

> him. But he only shouted louder, "Son of David, have mercy on me!"
>
> —Mark 10:47–48

Bartimaeus called Jesus the "Son of David." That's very interesting, isn't it? In fact, this is the *first* time in the Book of Mark that *anyone* calls Jesus this. Why? What did a blind guy know about Jesus that no one else did? And an even better question may be—what does that even *mean*?

Let's break this down piece by piece. First, what does it mean that Bartimaeus called Jesus the "Son of David"?

When someone shouted, "Son of David!" at Jesus, they weren't just tossing out a nickname. They were plugging Him straight into centuries of Messianic expectation. You see, every Jew knew the covenant promise. They had been looking for it—or, I should say, looking for *Him*.

In 2 Samuel 7:12–13 (esv), God told David, "I will raise up your offspring after you. . . .I will establish the throne of his kingdom forever." And that's not the only scripture they knew. They also would have remembered Isaiah 9:6–7, which says,

> For a child is born to us, a son is given to us. The government will rest on his shoulders. And he will be called: Wonderful Counselor, Mighty God, Everlasting Father, Prince of Peace. His government and its peace will never end. He will rule with fairness and justice from the throne of his ancestor David for all eternity. The passionate commitment of the Lord of Heaven's Armies will make this happen!

Not to mention, we have Jeremiah 23:5 (esv), which says, "I will raise up for David a righteous Branch, and he shall reign as king and deal wisely," and Ezekiel 34:23–24, where God says He will set up "my servant David" as shepherd over His people.

This is ground zero. In the Scriptures "Son of David" equals the Messiah. Every Jew knew the Messiah would come from David's line. So when Bartimaeus shouted, "Son of David, have mercy on me!" he was truly saying something!

"What was he saying *exactly*?"

I am so glad you asked! He was saying, "I know who You are!"

But wait just a second. Before we go any further, have you noticed anything strange yet? We keep asking, "Who do you say I am?" So we are starting to see the value in understanding not only the why but the who when it comes to relationships. So riddle me this, Batman: *Why* are we told *who* Bartimaeus is? Have you ever even thought about that at all? I hadn't—until I did.

I remember the night very well, actually. I had been studying this story to preach on it for a church service I was invited to. I wanted to understand the story to the best of my ability, so I decided to read the entire Book of Mark in one sitting to see whether anything else resonated with the story of Bartimaeus.

Here is what stuck out to me—there are thirteen distinct healing miracles recorded in Mark:

1. Unclean spirit in the synagogue (Mark 1:21–28)
2. Peter's mother-in-law (fever) (Mark 1:29–31)
3. Leper cleansed (Mark 1:40–45)
4. Paralytic lowered through the roof (Mark 2:1–12)
5. Man with a withered hand (Mark 3:1–6)
6. Gerasene demoniac (Legion) (Mark 5:1–20)
7. Woman with the issue of blood (Mark 5:25–34)
8. Jairus's daughter raised (Mark 5:21–24, 35–43)
9. Syrophoenician woman's daughter (Mark 7:24–30)
10. Deaf and mute man (Mark 7:31–37)

11. Blind man at Bethsaida (Mark 8:22–26)
12. Boy with unclean spirit (seizures) (Mark 9:14–29)
13. Blind Bartimaeus (Mark 10:46–52)

Are you tracking with me on this? Out of the thirteen specific healings in Mark, *only one person* is given a name: blind Bartimaeus.

Everyone else is either identified by condition (a leper, a paralytic, a deaf and mute man), by relationship (Jairus's daughter, Peter's mother-in-law), or not identified at all (a boy with an unclean spirit).

That led me to an even deeper dive. I decided to look at the healing miracles in all four Gospel accounts. It's like this in all of them! I counted forty-two healing miracles. (I had to take Algebra 1 all four years of high school, so don't take my count as gold!) Nevertheless, forty-two distinct, detailed healing miracles are recorded across the four Gospels. On top of that, there are at least a dozen-plus summary passages (like Matthew 4:24, Mark 1:32–34, and Luke 6:17–19) where Jesus heals crowds of people—way beyond counting. John even says, "Jesus did many other things as well. If every one of them were written down, I suppose that even the whole world would not have room for the books" (John 21:25, NIV).

Out of those forty-two healing miracles I counted, do you know how many times we are told people's names? Three.

Yep. Only three.

Bartimaeus (whom you know), Malchus (the servant whose ear Peter cut off, who was healed by Jesus), and Lazarus (who was raised from the dead).

Now I can understand that the anonymity keeps the focus on Jesus' authority and compassion, not on His celebrity patients. But when someone is named in the Bible, *whatever* the reason may be, it usually means *something*. They may have been well known in or by the early church (like Nicodemus, Gamaliel, or Jairus). Their story may have carried unique theological weight (such as in Lazarus's case). Or their name tied them into a bigger narrative (like Malchus, who was connected to the arrest of Jesus).

This makes Bartimaeus stand out. None of those reasons apply to him at all. That means there is something deeper hidden here. But what could it be?

I searched the Internet. Nothing. I asked other pastors who are friends of mine. Nada. I even asked ChatGPT! Zero for three. Finally, I asked God. (Why do we always make this our last option?) And if you have ever had the privilege of carrying on a conversation with the Lord, you already know where this is going.

God never gives a straight answer, does He? He always throws the ball back to *you*.

"God, uh—I'm stuck here. Why did You tell us Bartimaeus's name but hardly anyone else's name that You healed? What made *him* so special?"

One word. That's all I heard back: "*Bar.*"

"*Bar?* What do You mean, God? I need to go to a bar? Pretty sure I left that scene behind in 2013!" Just kidding. I knew what He meant. While going through Bible college, we had talked about this before. It was years ago, so I didn't catch it right away. But when God said, "Bar," it all came rushing back.

We see several people mentioned in the Bible who have *Bar-* at the start of their names. Simon Bar-Jonah (Matt. 16:17, ESV), Bar-Jesus (Acts 13:6–12, ESV), and Barnabas (Acts 11:25), just to name a few. You see, this doesn't mean Bartimaeus's name was Bart. *Bar* means "son of."

We never knew his name. We still don't. Only his father's: *Timaeus.*

And just like that, the plot thickens! "Blind Bartimaeus" just means "the blind son of Timaeus." So why would the Bible tell us his dad's name?

That is a great question. And in the next chapter, we are about to find out.

But first I want to challenge you: What do people really know you for? Your faith or your failures? Ask yourself: "If my story were dropped into Scripture, what would I be known as? Would I be remembered only by my weakness, like the blind man, the leper, the paralytic? Or would I be remembered by my recognition of Jesus—like Bartimaeus, the one who shouted, 'Son of David,' when no one else did or ever had?"

Write it down. Pray over it. And then ask God to reshape your identity so that when people remember your name, they remember the Jesus you cried out to instead.

To access more content from Kelly K, scan the QR code or visit KellyKBooks.com/believer/ch16.

CORTNEY ROE

I don't have a big miraculous testimony of going from a beggar to a believer, but what I do have is a closer relationship with God and a peace I didn't have before. I have a lot of health issues, including anxiety and overthinking. Now instead of begging God to help me and having anxiety attacks and no peace in my mind, I thank Him and trust Him that He's with me and everything is just fine. Then it is.

When I start thanking Him, it brings me into His presence, as Psalm 100:4 says. That's when the calm comes. I'm so grateful to God for using Kelly the way He is, opening my eyes to the truth of God's Word and who God truly is.

CHAPTER 17

THE KEYS ARE IN YOUR HAND

Sōzō (verb, Greek)

: to save, to heal, to rescue, to deliver, to make whole[1]

: to cure, heal, restore to health[2]

All right now, let's put the pieces together, shall we? Why in the world would Mark tell us Bartimaeus's dad's name when he didn't bother with the dozens of others Jesus healed? I mean, you don't see "Steve the leper" or "Rachel the paralytic" in the Gospels.

Nope. Just Bartimaeus—son of Timaeus.

That little detail should make our spiritual Spidey senses tingle. The Bible doesn't name-drop unless the name actually matters. And if it mattered enough to make the cut, then Timaeus wasn't just some random dude.

Now, this isn't Scripture—it's just me thinking out loud. I can't prove it to be true. But I can't prove it to be false either. Either way, here's what I believe: Timaeus was probably a Pharisee or a Sadducee. While there's no hard proof, many scholars believe that the names preserved in Scripture often pointed to social or religious significance.

Here is what I'm getting at. If Timaeus *was* a Pharisee or Sadducee, that would have made him a man who was soaked in the Scriptures, reading the prophecies of Isaiah and Jeremiah out loud, Sabbath after Sabbath. And guess who would've been sitting there, week after week, hearing those prophecies? His blind son.

If this *is* the case, suddenly Bartimaeus's cry makes perfect sense: "Son of David, have mercy on me!" (Mark 10:48). He wasn't pulling that out of thin air. He was pulling it out of everything he'd ever heard his father teach.

See what's happening here? The crowd tried to silence him, but Bartimaeus had the prophecies echoing in his heart. His father's words about the coming Messiah came alive the moment Jesus walked by. And he had the guts to shout it when no one else would.

Do you remember in chapter 8 when I told you that insight is greater than eyesight? This is what I was hinting at!

When it comes to our question, "Who do you say I am?" blind Bartimaeus may not have had the ability to see with his physical eyes, but he could absolutely see with his spiritual eyes! The simple truth of the matter is—what you *know* to be true in the Spirit will always be greater than what you can see with your eyes.

Bartimaeus was the first person in the Book of Mark to call Jesus the Son of David. Why? Because he had a revelation of who He was! And how did he get that revelation? By spending time in God's Word. This is why he knew what almost everyone else seemed to miss.

Most people were looking at Jesus and building their understanding of who He was based on what they could see. But Bartimaeus was looking at Jesus through the lens of what he already *knew*. He knew the prophecies because he spent time in Scripture. His perspective wasn't based on sight alone. So when he heard about Jesus, he put two and two together.

He said, "Wait a minute! I've heard about this man coming all my life! I may not be able to see, but I still know what I'm looking for. This is the Messiah! *This* is the Son of David!"

You see, you will never be able to answer the question, "Who do *you say* Jesus is?" with confidence until you actually know *who Jesus is* and *what He did for you*. This is why so many people are stuck saying beggar prayers every single day, frustrated that in their own lives they don't see or experience the God they hear about at church.

How can you say "thank You" for something you don't even know you've already received?

Let me show you something else that we tend to miss in this story—or even in the Bible in general. Mark 10:52 says, "And Jesus said to him, 'Go, for your faith has healed you.' Instantly the man could see, and he followed Jesus down the road." We have already looked at how it was his faith that healed him, but here is what I haven't shown you yet—the word *healed*.

It should come as no surprise when I tell you that the Bible wasn't written in English. The Old Testament was originally written in Hebrew and Aramaic. The New Testament was written in Greek. So what was the Greek word used here, where we see *healed*?

Sōzō.

So what Jesus actually said was, "Go, your faith has *sōzō*'d you." And why does that matter? I'll tell you!

We actually see the word *sōzō* used over one hundred times in the New Testament. But this is where it gets interesting. We see it in our story here, where it gets translated with the word *healed*, but it's also the word used in almost every other place we see the word *healed*. And even more amazing than that, we see it used in places where it is translated into the word *saved* or *salvation*, and also in places where it is translated as *delivered* or *rescued*!

- "He will save [*sōzō*] his people from their sins" (Matt. 1:21).
- "Such a prayer offered in faith will heal [*sōzō*] the sick" (Jas. 5:15).
- "Your faith has made you well [*sōzō*]" (Luke 8:48).

Are you picking up what I'm throwing down here? Do you see the bigger picture yet? I don't want to come right out and tell you.

I want the light bulb to click with your own understanding! So let me show you a few more verses, and you see whether you can figure out where we are going with all this:

> But God showed his great love for us by sending Christ to die for us while we were still sinners. And since we have been made right in God's sight by the blood of Christ, he will certainly save us from God's condemnation.
>
> —Romans 5:8–9

Greek verb σῴζω (*sōzō*): "save us."

> For God chose to save us through our Lord Jesus Christ, not to pour out his anger on us. Christ died for us so that, whether we are dead or alive when he returns, we can live with him forever.
>
> —1 Thessalonians 5:9–10

Greek verb σῴζω (*sōzō*): "save us."

> So that everyone who believes in him will not perish but have eternal life. God sent his Son…not to judge the world, but to save the world through him.
>
> —John 3:16–17

Greek verb σῴζω (*sōzō*): "save the world."

Please tell me you got it now! When Jesus died on the cross, He didn't just *save* you; He *sōzō*'d you! He didn't *just* pay for your salvation; He also paid for your deliverance and your healing! All three are placed into one. You can't have salvation without healing, and you can't have healing without deliverance!

This is why we say the *finished* work of the cross! *Jesus paid it all!*

I know—we've known Jesus paid it all *forever*. We say it, we sing it, we *know* that. But do we really? If we truly *know* that, why do we continue to beg God constantly for what we want and need? Why have we been praying, "God, heal Jimmy if it be Your will," like we don't *already* know the will of God when it comes to healing?

If I know Jimmy has been *sōzō*'d, that means Jesus bought his healing for him at the same time He bought his salvation! This is why we need to drop "if it be Your will" and just say, "Thank You!"

Let me make this easy to understand, and then we will move on.

I love motorcycles. I recently got a bike that I have wanted for as long as I have wanted bikes. It's a 2025 Kawasaki Ninja ZX14—and I *love* it. But let's say, hypothetically speaking of course, that I get into some massive financial bind and have to go down to the pawnshop and pawn my bike.

Now once it's there, it's locked up. I can't touch it. I can't ride it. I can't even *look* at it! I have no access at all. But then there's you.

You see me in a bind. You see me hurting and broken over it. And you love me! I may not be able to pay the debt, but you can. So that's exactly what you do. You drive down to the pawnshop, you pay the price I owe on the bike, and you drive straight over to my house. You are so excited to tell me about what you've done for me, not in order to brag or be prideful but simply because you just love me that much.

You walk up to my porch, ring the doorbell, and I open the door. You say, "Kelly! I love you, man! So much! I knew you weren't going to be able to pay the debt you owed for your motorcycle, so I went and paid it for you. The bike belongs to you!"

But *what if*.

What if every day after that, I drove to your house, walked up to your door, and rang the bell. And as soon as you answered, I started saying, "Can I have my motorcycle, please? Will you give me my bike now? I really want it. I *need* it, actually. Can I have it, please?"

That would be absolutely ridiculous, right?

At some point you would *have* to look at me and say, "*Kelly!*

Bro! It's already been bought and paid for, my man. It's yours! Just go get it!"

And right there we have it. The exact scenario we find most Christians living in for their entire lives. Everything they need, want, or ever could imagine has *already* been bought and paid for them. Their healing, deliverance, finances, marriage, kids—all paid for. It's done. But instead of going to get it by thanking God that it's theirs, they keep begging God over and over for what already belongs to them.

Is that you? Or should I say, *was* that you?

Because from this moment on, it won't be. It can't be. You will never be able to beg and plead with God again. Because now you know the transaction is done!

We need to ditch the lie or half-truth that Jesus paid for your salvation, gave you access to His Father, and made a way for you to spend eternity with Him—but the sickness? The diagnosis? The poverty? The addiction? Yeah, you just have to live with those. But heaven is going to be awesome!

Yeah, I don't think so.

Remember when we started this book? I told you the faith it takes to believe Jesus paid for your salvation is the same faith it takes to see someone healed. That means *you* too.

Here's the bottom line: *Sōzō* isn't a cute theological buzzword you whisper at the altar. It's a verb. It's a finished transaction. When Jesus said, "Your faith has *sōzō*'d you," He wasn't hinting. He was handing you the receipt.

If Bartimaeus could hear his father's Scripture-soaked sermons and call Jesus the Son of David without seeing a single thing, you can believe the finished work with your eyes closed and your hands open.

The difference between a beggar and a believer isn't more pleading; it's knowing. Knowledge births boldness. Boldness births action. Action looks like faith that walks, not wishing that waits at the curb begging.

So what do you do now? I'll tell you!

Stop treating the gospel like a future promise, and start treating it like a present possession. Stop rehearsing lack, and start saying *thank You*! When the old habit of begging creeps in, remind yourself: The debt's paid, the bike's in your garage, and the keys are in your hand.

Sōzō isn't pending. It's complete. Stop staring at the keys. Start the engine, and let's go ride!

To access more content from Kelly K, scan the QR code or visit KellyKBooks.com/believer/ch17.

LEAH PRICE

Seventeen years ago I completely lost all vision in my right eye. Two years ago the same thing came back and attacked my left eye, leaving me with 10 to 15 percent vision in that eye. It's like seeing through a cloudy shower door at all times. Shortly after the vision loss, my husband packed his bags and left.

I was born again only five years ago. I had been on fire for the kingdom for only three years when my eyesight was stolen from me. My prayers were a mess—all over the place. I went from begging God to take my life, to manipulating Him, to bargaining, to ultimately kick-starting my faith walk.

For an entire year, I begged God to heal me. Thanking Him, praising Him, and worshipping Him were game changers! If we believe the Bible is the infallible Word of God, then the promises for healing are for us too! Without a doubt I know my healing is coming! I know that. But even if it doesn't, *that's OK too*! You see, you can put your faith in the wrong thing, and it'll keep you a prisoner in your own mind.

But when you put your faith in Jesus and hold Him to His promises? Life-changing!

PART III
LIVE IT OUT

CHAPTER 18

WHO NEEDS TO BE HEALED?

Authority (noun)
: the power or right to give orders, make decisions, and enforce obedience[1]
: power to influence or command thought, opinion, or behavior

YOU THOUGHT BARTIMAEUS getting his sight was the end of the story, didn't you? Cute little miracle. Blind guy sees. Everybody claps. Cue the credits.

Nope. Not even close.

Mark didn't drop Bartimaeus in there just so we could post a feel-good devo on Instagram. This wasn't a random healing on Jesus' busy calendar. This was a spotlight, a setup, a divine mic drop to expose something deeper. Because let's be real—Bartimaeus wasn't the only blind one in that story.

Yeah, he couldn't see with his eyes, but at least he could see with his spirit. Meanwhile, you've got disciples who literally walked side by side with Jesus—watched Him feed thousands, calm storms, cast out demons—and they were still squinting like, "Uh, who is this guy again?"

So here's the punch line, my friend: Sometimes the blind guy yelling on the roadside has more sight than the crowd following right behind Jesus. Which begs the question, "Who really needs to be healed here?" And that is the third question we have been working toward.

This is where it's going to get uncomfortably close to home for some people. Because you and I? We're church kids, right? We've got Bibles on our phones, verses in our heads, sermons in our ears. But if all we've got is head knowledge and zero revelation, we're just as blind as the crowd trying to shush Bartimaeus.

This isn't about shame. It's about sight. And thank God, He still opens eyes.

You see, physical blindness wasn't the real issue in Mark 10. Blind Bartimaeus *knew* he was going to be healed before Jesus even called him over! Spiritual blindness is the real issue in this story.

Bartimaeus couldn't see a thing, but he knew the Messiah when He walked by. Meanwhile, the religious folks with two good eyes were too busy managing the moment to recognize the miracle.

Oh? What's that? You didn't know the crowd of people telling Bartimaeus to be quiet were actually the disciples and Jesus' other followers? That's OK! I didn't either at first. But as I began to study this story in multiple translations and commentaries, that fact became crystal clear.

You see, this wasn't just a regular day when Jesus and the disciples were out for a stroll. They were actually on their way to an event—and not just *any* event. Passover. That would be like the Super Bowl of Jewish festivals. It was a big deal.

Remember when I said that it wasn't a coincidence that Jesus asked the disciples, "Who do you say I am?" *before* they got to Bartimaeus? This is why I think that. He was preparing them for this moment. I believe He was checking to see whether they understood the heart of His Father yet. And they missed it!

In the story of Bartimaeus, the disciples and Jesus' other followers simply saw Jesus as a religious figure who needed to do "religious figure things." That meant Passover took priority over a blind beggar. But was that *really* the case?

What does God care about more? Events or people?

Exactly! People! James 1:18 says, "He chose to give birth to us by giving us his true word. And we, out of all creation, became his prized possession." *We* are God's prized possessions! Not temples, not shrines, not statues, not government systems, or even religious doctrines. And definitely not events and ceremonies.

Jesus wanted them to understand God's heart for people, and all through the Book of Mark, He was showing them that very thing. They just kept missing it! Over and over again in Mark, Jesus brought the focus back to people—and He did it with authority. He showed that He has authority over identity, over spirits and nature, over sin, and over the Law.

Jesus was not only exercising authority *within* the Law, but He was also stepping *above* it. He claimed the divine right to reveal its true meaning: that God cares about *people*! It's like He was saying, "You've been reading the footnotes; I *wrote* the book." Let's look at the following examples of this.

Sabbath controversy (Mark 2:23–28): The disciples picked grain on the Sabbath; the Pharisees freaked out. Jesus answered, "The Son of Man is Lord, even over the Sabbath!" (v. 28). That's not just a rule-bending statement—that's Him claiming authority over one of the Ten Commandments and revealing what those commandments were always meant to be about.

Healing on the Sabbath (Mark 3:1–6): Jesus healed a man's withered hand in the synagogue. He reframed the law: "Does the law permit good deeds on the Sabbath, or is it a day for doing evil? Is this a day to save life or to destroy it?" (v. 4). He was not abolishing the Sabbath; He was interpreting the true heart of it: people!

Purity laws (Mark 7:1–23): The Pharisees complained about handwashing. Jesus said it's not what goes into a person that defiles them, but what comes out of the heart. Mark even comments, "By saying this, he declared that every kind of food is acceptable in God's eyes" (v. 19). That's an *earthquake* in Jewish legal categories. Jesus has the authority to define what's clean and unclean—and it isn't about stuff. It's about the heart—about people!

That's the point everyone was missing, including the disciples. All the rules (the laws) and the religious ceremonies and festivals carried the same purpose: to point back to the loving heart of the Father! Because *none* of our walk with God is about what we *do*. It's about what Jesus did, what you believe about God, and who He is to you!

When you feel like you have to earn your place with Him, you will be chained to a list of rules to make you feel like you *deserve* to be close to Him. But the reality of the situation is that Jesus followed all the rules for you because you were *never* going to be able to!

Now you can just be as close as you want to the Father and His heart because your proximity to God was never about *you* anyway.

Mark wasn't just telling stories; he was setting patterns. Most of the big key moments that we read about actually happened twice. There are two feeding miracles in Mark 6:30–44 and Mark 8:1–10:

1. Feeding the five thousand (mostly a Jewish crowd)
2. Feeding the four thousand (mostly a Gentile crowd)

Same miracle, different audience. This shows us that Jesus' authority extends to all people. There were also two boat and storm incidents, covered in Mark 4:35–41 and Mark 6:45–52:

1. He calms the storm with a word.
2. He walks on water and reveals His divine identity.

The repetition highlights the disciples' ongoing struggle to get it. The "twiceness" underscores the disciples' dullness, Jesus' authority, and the widening scope of His mission. But wait, there's more!

There is another instance of the same thing happening twice in Mark. Let's go back to Mark 8, two chapters before we get to our story of blind Bartimaeus in Mark 10:

> When they arrived at Bethsaida, some people brought a blind man to Jesus, and they begged him to touch the man and heal him. Jesus took the blind man by the hand and led him out of the village. Then, spitting on the man's eyes, he laid his hands on him and asked, "Can you see anything now?" The man looked around. "Yes," he said, "I see people, but I can't see them very clearly. They look like trees walking around." Then Jesus placed his hands on the man's eyes again, and his eyes were opened. His sight was completely restored, and he could see everything clearly. Jesus sent him away, saying, "Don't go back into the village on your way home."
>
> —MARK 8:22–26

Are you kidding me? Literally two chapters before we get to blind Bartimaeus, we have Jesus healing a blind man! Are you feeling how thick the irony is here? They get to blind Bart, and they see a blind guy begging. In my opinion, knowing Jesus *just* healed a blind man, I would start shouting, "Jesus! Yo! Here's another one! You've done this before. We've seen it with our own eyes!"

But what do the disciples do instead? They try to shut him up, to tell him to be quiet. *Don't bother Jesus.*

They missed it.

But before we go further on that point, let's look back to the healing of the blind man in Mark 8. There is more going on here than Jesus needing two swings to hit a home run. I mean, you were wondering that, right? "Why didn't Jesus heal the man completely the first time?"

Jesus never accidentally underhealed anyone. He could have restored this man's vision instantly, no question. So why this two-stage healing? Let's break this down. Sometimes physical or spiritual healing happens in stages. Jesus was modeling that the kingdom doesn't always crash in all at once. God's work often unfolds progressively, sharpening vision step-by-step.

Jesus didn't need a second try. Mark has already shown Jesus healing with a word, a touch, and even at a distance. This is intentional. When Jesus asked, "Can you see anything now?" it's not because He was unsure. He was teaching the man (and the disciples watching) that sight is a journey. It was a test of the man's revelation, not Jesus' performance. It's almost like He was saying, "Tell Me what you're experiencing. Where are you in your faith?"

Just like we learned with Bartimaeus, Jesus is looking for what you *believe* about who He is. But this miracle wasn't just personal; it was prophetic. Mark uses many miracles as living parables, and this one was a direct setup for what happened next—Peter's confession in Mark 8:29:

> Then he asked them, "But who do you say I am?" Peter replied, "You are the Messiah."

The disciples had "seen" Jesus feed thousands, calm storms, and even walk on water. But their vision was blurry. They saw something divine in Him but not with clarity. They'd seen the power but not the person. The miracles were in focus, but the Messiah was still blurry.

Only later, through the cross and resurrection, would their vision sharpen into a full understanding of who He is and what He came to do. This healing in Mark 8, then, is a prophetic symbol: first blurry faith, then clear revelation.

And here's where I'm going to flip the table on us: What if that's us today?

What if we've gotten so good at "doing church" that we've gone blind to the Christ we claim to follow? What if our vision is crystal clear when it comes to lights, logos, and lives, but we're totally blind when it comes to mercy, power, and actually trusting the One we're singing about?

Bartimaeus got his sight, but maybe we're the ones who need the healing.

And here is the clincher: You don't need permission to be healed; Jesus already paid for it and gave you the authority to go get it. You just need to open your eyes and walk in it.

To access more content from Kelly K, scan the QR code or visit KellyKBooks.com/believer/ch18.

VALERIE BROWN

Many years ago I was a single mother of three. My oldest son was seven, my daughter was three, and my youngest son was one. I had no money for a Thanksgiving dinner for my children, so I went to a church to ask for help. I expected a small turkey and maybe some potatoes. What I received was everything I needed to make a full Thanksgiving dinner and then some. I mean potatoes, sweet potatoes, green beans, and pumpkin pie, as well as toilet paper, paper towels, and several other basic household items that I definitely needed.

I had been praying to God for help with my rent for the next month because Christmas was coming and I had a choice to make. I pay the rent, or I have Christmas presents for my children. I couldn't do both. I thought to myself, "How do I tell my children Santa isn't coming to our house?"

Well, my God is so great! The church family who had brought all the amazing things for Thanksgiving called me a few days after the holiday to check in. I was in tears telling them how much I appreciated what they had done so my kids could have a great Turkey Day dinner. The mother told me during that conversation that their family was blessed by God and they always liked to pay it forward. She then continued to say that each year, they chose a family to help at Christmas, and this year they had chosen my children and me. My eyes are welling up just thinking about it now. She said they were paying my rent for the month of December and bringing gifts for the children. My God not only knew my need but supplied an abundance of it. This absolutely took me from a beggar to a believer.

CHAPTER 19

EYES ON THE FATHER

Cataract (noun)

: a clouding of the lens of the eye

: an age-related or medically induced condition in which proteins in the eye's lens clump together, causing the lens to become cloudy and reducing the sharpness of vision[1]

OK, HERE'S WHERE things get uncomfortably ironic. Again, the very people trying to keep Bartimaeus quiet weren't Pharisees. They weren't Roman guards. They weren't random hecklers on the side of the road.

Nope. It was the disciples. The Jesus followers. The "in crowd."

The ones who should have been first in line to cheer on a miracle were the first ones to muzzle it. And that's where the story flips on its head.

Because Bartimaeus's blindness was obvious. You could see it in his eyes. You could hear it in his begging. But the blindness of the disciples? That's the kind you don't notice until Jesus exposes it.

The physical healing in this story is just the surface. The deeper issue, the one we've all got to wrestle with, is the spiritual healing needed by the people who thought they were already fine. That's why this isn't just a story about Bartimaeus finally seeing. It's about us realizing how often *we* don't.

It's about asking every single day, "Who needs to be healed?"

Because sometimes it's the broken world around us—and sometimes it's us.

The disciples weren't telling Bartimaeus to shut up because they were villains. They weren't trying to be cruel. They were trying to be practical. "We've got a schedule, Jesus. We've got an event to get to. We've got Passover coming up—the biggest deal of the year. No time for side quests. No time for beggars in the ditch."

Here's the sting: Whenever following Jesus turns into managing Jesus, we've already gone blind. The second His presence becomes an inconvenience, we've missed the heart of the Father.

The truth is, the disciples' vision was blurred by spiritual cataracts. They thought they were helping Jesus by silencing Bartimaeus. They thought they were protecting Jesus' time. In reality, they were resisting the very heart of God. Jesus didn't need protection. He needed followers who could see the Father's priorities.

And isn't that us sometimes?

We know the verses. We show up for the services. We've got the rhythm of Christianity down cold. But then somebody inconvenient cries out for mercy, and we treat it like background noise. Someone's need bumps up against our schedule, our vibe, our "Passover plans." Suddenly, we're the ones telling Bartimaeus to be quiet.

The danger isn't being blind like Bart. The danger is thinking you can see when you're actually just walking in circles, missing the point. And what is the point? That's the question your soul has to answer every day.

The point is keeping your eyes on the Father.

Sounds basic, not life-changing. But what if it is?

Let me show you how deep this really goes. But first, let me remind you of our three main questions we have been looking at—the questions we need to start asking ourselves every day:

- Am I a beggar or a believer?
- Who do you say I am?
- Who needs to be healed?

We have already discussed each of these questions in detail. But now let me show you the why behind them.

Each one, without you even being aware of it, is shifting your focus from you—your situation, your opinions, other people, work, you name it—back to the Father.

- "Beggar or believer?" *Where is my trust?*
- "Who do I say He is?" *Where is my identity?*
- "Who needs to be healed?" *Where is my compassion, my heart?*

Every question forces me to take my eyes off myself and put them back on the Father. That's the why. And here's the wild part. Every rule, law, and commandment in the Bible is doing the exact same thing! Not just controlling your behavior. Not just keeping you in check. Not just giving you a holy to-do list so you can feel smug when you check the boxes. Nope.

Every single question is pulling your eyes off yourself and fixing them back where they belong: on the Father. Think about it: "Don't murder" doesn't just mean stop short of stabbing somebody. It means deal with the hate brewing in your heart before it poisons you. And how do you do that? By shifting your focus from how *you* feel about them to "Father, how do *You* feel about them?"

"Don't commit adultery" isn't just about avoiding an affair. It's about refusing to let lust colonize your soul and drag your eyes away from God's design. Even the "random" commands—like dietary laws or festivals—weren't arbitrary. They were constant reminders that life wasn't about Israel's cravings, comfort, or calendar. It was about God's holiness, God's provision, God's rhythm.

The rules were never just about rules. They were about refocusing. They were soul alignment tools. Divine eye exams. Every commandment is basically God whispering, "Hey, stop staring at yourself. Look at Me."

Here's where it gets brutal. When we treat God's commands like behavior management, we miss the point entirely. The point isn't modification; it's transformation. Not sin control, but soul renewal.

That's why Jesus could stand and deliver the Sermon on the Mount and say, "You've heard it said…but I say to you…" He wasn't rewriting the law; He was revealing its depth. He was showing that the law had always been less about what your hands do and more about where your heart looks.

This is why I am always teaching, "It's not about the what; it's about the why!"

So this is it. Every law, every command, every rule? They're not shackles. They're sight givers. They strip away the cataracts of selfishness, self-sufficiency, and self-focus so we can finally see the Father clearly. Each command clears the fog. Each one peels off another layer of blindness. They weren't chains to carry; they were lenses to finally see what matters.

The thing about the law is that it can show you you're blind, but it can't make you see. It's like a mirror. You look into it, and suddenly, all the smudges, all the dirt, all the cataracts are obvious. But a mirror doesn't clean your face. It just shows you the mess. That's what the commandments do: They reveal blindness. They expose the heart that keeps wandering off course. They strip away every excuse until you can't pretend anymore.

But if all you've got is law, you're stuck staring at your own blindness, with no way out. That's why grace is everything. Grace doesn't just point out the problem; grace *restores sight*. Grace is the lens cleaner, the cataract remover, the divine hand that reaches into your soul and does what rules never could.

Bartimaeus crying out? That was the law at work. It revealed his condition, his desperate need, his utter dependence. But Jesus stopping in His tracks? That was grace stepping in.

The law exposed his blindness, but grace gave him his healing. The law showed him how bad off he was, but grace let him walk away seeing for the first time. And that's the rhythm of the kingdom: The law opens our eyes to the fact that we're blind. Grace gives us eyes that finally see. Because the law wasn't written to create perfect little robots who never mess up. It was written to expose our blindness—to yank our focus off our hustle, our plans, our Passover schedules—and lock our focus back on the Father.

Bartimaeus got his sight back that day. But the disciples? They got a wake-up call.

Bart knew he was blind. That's why he cried out. The disciples didn't know they were blind. That's why they tried to shut him up. And that's the razor's edge every single one of us has to walk.

"Am I the believer thanking God for meeting my needs before I see it? Or am I the 'follower' who's actually too busy chasing my own agenda to see the Father right in front of me?"

The commandments scream it. The rules whisper it. The entire Word of God pounds it into the ground: "Eyes on the Father." Not eyes on your success. Not eyes on your failures. Not eyes on your enemies. Not even eyes on your ministry.

Eyes. On. The. Father.

That's where the real miracle is. That's where the blindness lifts. That's where the soul transformation begins. When your eyes lock on Him, you stop managing Jesus and you actually start following Him. And following Jesus means stepping out of your agenda and stepping into His authority.

Then suddenly, just like Bartimaeus, you can see.

To access more content from Kelly K, scan the QR code or visit KellyKBooks.com/believer/ch19.

ANN AND DON SWOPE

Don has been riding the roller coaster with his mobility issues. We were at the point where I truly said, "God, here or in heaven, I believe *You* are healing him." Leah prayed for us over the phone, and within a few days, God had him on a much-improved journey. He was doing so well that his nurse pushed him to do more, and we lost ground again. But we keep praising through! He is now improving again—slow and steady. We won't be pushing too hard.

Another part of the praise is we have someone who is like a daughter to us and has struggled with addiction. She is now six months clean and is Don's caregiver, so I can return to work after a six-week leave to help him. Our faith and trust in God has also opened her boyfriend's heart. Seeing faith in action made him start to be more open to seeing how God works when we give *Him* access and control!

CHAPTER 20

THE ROOT AND THE FRUIT

Rebellion (noun)

: opposition to one in authority or dominance

: open, armed, and usually unsuccessful defiance of or resistance to an established government

NOW LET'S TAKE this to the next level. Why does it seem like keeping our eyes on the Father is one of the most difficult tasks in the world?

We don't stumble because we aren't trying hard enough. We stumble because we're staring at the wrong thing. You can spend all day grinding away—trying to fix your habits, wrestle your temptations, and white-knuckle your way out of sin. But if your eyes are still locked on *you*, you'll never win. Why? Because you're still the one holding the scalpel—and self can't cut out self.

The real issue isn't the fruit. It's the root. You can spray poison on the fruit all day long, but if you don't dig out the root, it's just going to grow back nastier. And the root of every sin is the *exact* same. Think about it.

Lucifer's fall was cosmic—not because he hated heaven but because his view of the throne of heaven shifted. He saw it no longer as *God's* throne but as the one he wanted for himself.

Adam and Eve's fall was historic. They ate not because the fruit was filling but because their eyes moved from their Creator to their craving. And the world still groans under the weight of that glance.

Israel's fall was national. They danced before golden calves—not because gold gleamed brighter than glory but because they dropped their gaze from the God who split seas to gods they could hammer with their own hands. It cost them forty years in the wilderness.

And our fall? It's personal. We don't burn out because ministry is too heavy. We burn out because our gaze drifts. We keep hacking at fruit—better sermons, longer hours, stricter rules—but the root remains untouched: eyes off Him, eyes on us. Every sin, every failure, every single time you and I cave to temptation—it doesn't start with the act. It starts with a glance. A shift of focus. A gaze gone rogue.

That's why "eyes on the Father" isn't just a catchy slogan. It's survival. Because the moment your focus drifts, the root starts growing. And the longer your eyes wander, the deeper it digs.

Now let me show you the why behind all this and exactly how deep this rabbit hole really goes.

If I were to ask you, "What was the *first* sin ever committed?" what would you say? Would you say Adam and Eve eating the fruit? You would be right if I had asked what the first sin *humans* committed was. But was that the *first* sin? No. We already know that Lucifer sinned first.

> How you are fallen from heaven, O shining star, son of the morning! You have been thrown down to the earth, you who destroyed the nations of the world. For you said to yourself, "I will ascend to heaven and set my throne above God's stars. I will preside on the mountain of the gods far away in the north. I will climb to the highest heavens and be like the Most High."
>
> —Isaiah 14:12–14

So what was the sin? "Easy, Kelly! Pride! He decided that he was going to be greater than God. That's pride all day long!"

Sure, pride was there. But pride is never the starting point. It's only the fruit. Something deeper was already in the soil. Come on, friend—dig deeper!

Pride doesn't just show up out of nowhere. Just like no one wakes up and decides, "I'm going to cheat on my spouse today! I've never thought about that before, but today—I'm going to do it!" Affairs start with a thought that led to a conversation that led to an emotional connection that led to a decision that led to an action.

Are you getting it? Pride, lust, greed, envy, murder, and so on are all just *fruit* that appear when we are connected to the wrong *root*. This is why saying pride was the first sin is actually incredibly dangerous. Because it isn't the root, the *cause*. It's just the fruit, a *symptom*. And if we try to kill the root by spraying chemicals on the fruit, that's like taking a cough drop to cure cancer. It's not going to work.

So what was the first sin?

Rebellion.

That is the root that all other fruit (sin) grows out of. Now it makes sense that God's *first* command to humanity was all about focus. In the garden He didn't start with a long list of rules. He gave Adam and Eve one clear command: "Don't eat from that tree" (Gen. 2:16–17, paraphrased). That wasn't about fruit—it was about focus. God was saying, "Keep your eyes on Me. Trust My word above everything else." Later, He made it even louder in Deuteronomy 6:4–5:

> Listen, O Israel! The Lord is our God, the Lord alone. And you must love the Lord your God with all your heart, all your soul, and all your strength.

That's not part-time loyalty. That's full focus—heart, soul, strength. *Everything on Him.* And that's why rebellion is the ugliest sin in the book—because rebellion is simply choosing *not* to focus on God. It's saying, "I hear You, Lord, but I'll do my own thing." That's the heartbeat of every fall: from Lucifer in heaven to Adam in Eden, to Israel in the wilderness, to you and me today.

And God doesn't play games with rebellion. Look at 1 Samuel 15:23: "Rebellion is as sinful as witchcraft, and stubbornness as bad as worshiping idols." Think about that. God puts rebellion in the same category as witchcraft and idolatry. That's not a slip of the pen—that's a divine warning. Rebellion isn't just breaking a rule; it's breaking a relationship. It's ripping your eyes off the Father and fixing them on yourself.

Proverbs doesn't soften the blow either: "Evil people are eager for rebellion, but they will be severely punished" (Prov. 17:11). Or how about Ezekiel, where God calls out Israel: "But they rebelled against me and would not listen. They did not get rid of the vile images they were obsessed with, or forsake the idols of Egypt" (Ezek. 20:8).

These moments of rebellion? They're what give birth to pride. Not the other way around. Rebellion is the root, and every other sin is just the rotten fruit hanging off its branches.

I mean, look at David! Even through all his failures, he kept coming back as a man after God's own heart. Not because he never sinned but because his gaze always returned. His strength wasn't that he never lost focus but that he never let rebellion have the last word.

At the beginning of this chapter, I told you I'd show you why it's so hard to keep our focus on God. *This* is the reason. Instead of working on where our eyes and heart are focused, we keep turning inward, trying to hack away at the fruit: lust, pride, greed, anger, envy, whatever. But no matter how hard we swing at the fruit, the root keeps feeding it—and the root is rebellion.

Rebellion doesn't always look like a fist shaken in God's face. Sometimes it's subtle. Sometimes it looks like good intentions gone rogue. "I'll fix myself. I'll do better next time. I'll try harder." But if your gaze is on you, not Him, it's still rebellion.

Sometimes rebellion looks like religion without Him.

Sometimes it looks like praying but only so you feel better. Sometimes it looks like serving but secretly craving the spotlight.

Focus is worship. The moment your eyes drift from His glory, you've already bowed to something else.

It's still the first domino—the starting point of every fall. The solution isn't sin management. The solution is surrender: eyes locked on Jesus, rooted in His Spirit, walking in His strength.

And here's the best part: Once you surrender, once you stop fighting to fix yourself, and let Christ live through you—everything shifts. That's where we're headed next. Because when He lives through us, we stop living like a cup always desperate to be filled and start living like a hose always pouring out.

And here's the beautiful irony: The hose never runs dry. The hose always stays wet.

So let's turn the page because in the next chapter, we're about to discover what it means to stop chasing our own fullness and start living as the hands and feet of Jesus: the very conduits of His promises to the world.

To access more content from Kelly K, scan the QR code or visit KellyKBooks.com/believer/ch20.

SCOTT RAPER, PART 2

Charlie Kirk was a believer in Christ who was not ashamed of telling the truth and love of our Savior. On September 10, 2025, he was shot and killed in front of a nation—an unforgettable episode in history. I was a paramedic working on the ambulance that day. I will always remember this tragic incident—same as remembering where you were when you saw the towers fall.

That night, I was driving home, listening to Pastor Luke talk about this. I remember looking up at the night sky and starting to pray,

thanking God for the love He has for Charlie's family, for the people who were there and saw what happened, for our nation, for the world.

When I was a young kid, I asked God for the gift of tongues, thinking that it would be cool. I didn't really know what it was. As Kelly is fond of saying, "Buckle up, buttercup!"

I can remember hearing Luke's voice get further away from me. I felt a hum in my mouth, my tongue, as a singsong sound came from my mouth. I wasn't there, but I was there. I could see myself. I could see a light and a wall of sand-colored brick. I knew I was at the wailing wall. I could feel the bricks and the sun on my skin. And all I could hear was the singsong prayer coming out of my mouth.

I knew what I was saying, but I don't know what it was now. The next thing I remember is hearing Luke's voice over the podcast coming back on. I was parked in my driveway at home. My commute is about an hour, and when I looked at my phone, the podcast had only been on for about ten minutes.

I know in my heart I had an encounter with the Holy Spirit—a very powerful, purposeful one. One that shows what can be done when you let the Holy Spirit and the Father in your life and you follow Their lead and don't try to lead Them. I know my journey is just starting, and I am honestly very excited and blessed to see where He takes me. I know it is better than anything I could imagine.

CHAPTER 21

ARE YOU A CUP OR A HOSE?

Hose (noun)

: a flexible tube for conveying a liquid, as water, to a desired point[1]

Hose (verb)

: to water, wash, spray, or drench by means of a hose[2]

SO HERE WE are. Full surrender. Eyes off ourselves. Eyes locked on Jesus. And now everything changes.

See, this is where most believers stop. They think the Christian life is just about keeping their own cup full. "God, give me peace. God, give me joy. God, give me strength. God, fill me up." And yeah, He will—but that's not the point. Where is the focus?

Exactly. On us. Again. Already. So soon—*ouch.*

The truth of the matter is this, my friend: You weren't designed to be a cup. You were designed to be a hose. A cup just sits there, waiting to be filled, staring at itself, getting depressed by its lack.

A hose, on the other hand, stays connected to the source, and because it's connected, it never runs dry. A hose doesn't worry about being filled; it exists to pour out. And the crazy thing is, the hose always gets wet in the process. That's the mindset shift that flips everything.

When your life stops being about saying, "God, give me what I need," and starts being about saying, "God, flow through me to help others," that's when all the promises you've read about start exploding in your life. Because His heart has always been about people—and He wants to reach them through you.

Jesus said it this way: "Anyone who believes in me may come and drink! For the Scriptures declare, 'Rivers of living water will flow from his heart'" (John 7:38).

Catch that? He didn't say you'll just *hold* living water; He said it will *flow out of you*. That's hose language all day long. Paul backs this up in Galatians 2:20:

> My old self has been crucified with Christ. It is no longer I who live, but Christ lives in me. So I live in this earthly body by trusting in the Son of God, who loved me and gave himself for me.

Translation? The hose doesn't produce the water; it just carries it. Christ lives through you. You're just the conduit. And when you live like that, suddenly all those promises you've underlined in your Bible start popping off the page into your real life. Why? Because you've stopped obsessing over your own cup and started focusing on His flow.

Jesus told His disciples in Matthew 10:8, "Give as freely as you have received!" That works only if you're living like a hose. If you're just a cup, you'll always feel empty and stingy. But if you're a hose, you're constantly connected to the source, so you can give freely without fear of running dry.

This is the kingdom flip: When you focus on pouring out, He guarantees you'll always be filled. The flow never runs dry.

God calls us to be the hands and feet of Jesus. And what did Jesus do? He took care of people. How? In any way they needed. Hungry crowds? He fed them. Blind eyes? He opened them. Broken hearts? He healed them. That's who He is. That's what He does.

And here's the wild part: That's God's promise for us too! Over and over the Word calls Him a God of abundance, a God of more than enough:

> The LORD is my shepherd; I have all that I need.
>
> —PSALM 23:1

> And God will generously provide all you need. Then you will always have everything you need and plenty left over to share with others.
>
> —2 CORINTHIANS 9:8

> My purpose is to give them a rich and satisfying life.
>
> —JOHN 10:10

So why don't most believers experience that more-than-enough life? Not because God doesn't want to give it—He already promised it—but because of our focus.

Think about it: How many people in a cemetery are stressing about rent or bills? None. They're dead. And so are we. Romans 6:11 says we're dead to sin but alive to God. Dead people don't worry about themselves, so we don't have to either. Our eyes stay on Him. If I'm dead, I don't need to worry about my needs. Dead men don't stress about bills. Dead women don't panic about tomorrow. If I don't have to worry about me, then I don't have to *focus* on me. I can keep my eyes on God. And when my focus is on Him, His life flows through me.

The truth is, the moment you let go of trying to manage your own life and stop trying to manage God in your life—that's the moment He finally can. Jesus put it bluntly in Luke 9:24: "If you try to hang on to your life, you will lose it. But if you give up your life for my sake, you will save it."

God is a gentleman. If you want to build your own life, fight your own battles, stress about your own future—He'll let you. But if you surrender? If you take your hands off your life and start using them to build others? That's when God Himself steps in. That's when He fights for you. That's when He builds what you could never build.

This has been God's heart from the very beginning. When He called Abraham, He didn't just say, "I'll bless you." He went further:

> I will make you into a great nation. I will bless you and make you famous, and you will be a blessing to others. I will bless those who bless you and curse those who treat you with contempt. All the families on earth will be blessed through you.
>
> —Genesis 12:2–3

Did you catch that? God didn't promise Abraham blessings so he could sit back and sip from a golden cup. He promised blessings so that the entire world could drink from the overflow. He was a hose, not a cup.

And Paul tells us in Galatians 3:29, "And now that you belong to Christ, you are the true children of Abraham. You are his heirs, and God's promise to Abraham belongs to you." That means this promise isn't just ancient history; it's your inheritance. The same God who said, "I'll bless you so you can bless others," is saying the same thing to you right now.

If you're not seeing abundance, maybe it's not that God isn't pouring; it's that you're still trying to live like a cup instead of a hose. The blessing was never meant to stay with you. It was meant to move through you.

And here's the beautiful irony: When you finally live like a hose, when you finally surrender and let Him flow through you to others, you end up more satisfied, more supplied, and more secure than you ever were while chasing your own needs.

Jesus made it clear in both Matthew and Mark: The Son of Man didn't come to be served, but to serve—and to give His life as a ransom for many. That's the hose life He modeled for us.

And if that weren't enough, Jesus literally bent down, picked up a towel, and washed His disciples' dirty feet.

> And since I, your Lord and Teacher, have washed your feet, you ought to wash each other's feet. I have given you an example to follow. Do as I have done to you.
>
> —John 13:14–15

This is what it means to be the hands and feet of Jesus: to step into the dirt, the mess, the need, and let His Spirit flow through us in practical, selfless, sacrificial ways. When you do, something shifts. You stop chasing the promises of God and start living in them—because His promises were never designed to fill cups. They were designed to flow through hoses.

Here's the reality: God doesn't just want to bless *you*. He wants to bless people *through* you. He doesn't just want to meet your needs; He wants to make you a channel to meet the needs of others. And the more you pour out, the more you discover the truth: The hose always gets wet. This is the abundant life Jesus promised.

But here's the rub: Not many will ever experience it. Not because God doesn't want them to but because they're chasing the wrong thing.

Jesus said in Matthew 7:14, "But the gateway to life is very narrow and the road is difficult, and only a few ever find it." That's not just about heaven someday; that's about life *now.* Few find abundant life because they're searching for life instead of keeping their eyes on the life giver.

So as we close this chapter, remember: You weren't called to be a cup. You were called to be a hose. Stay connected to the source. Let Him flow through you. Take your eyes off yourself, and fix them on Him.

Because the narrow road to life isn't found by chasing blessings. It's found by chasing Jesus.

To access more content from Kelly K, scan the QR code or visit KellyKBooks.com/believer/ch21.

AYLA ANDERSON

I never thought God would reach me the way He did. For the longest time, I carried around fear—fear of the future, fear of loss, fear of not being enough. I knew about God, but I didn't know Him personally. My life felt like it was hanging together by threads, and I kept asking silently, "Lord, if You're real, show me."

Then one day, I started noticing something strange. Psalm 91 kept appearing in front of me. First, it was on a random post I scrolled past on social media. A few days later, an Uber driver was listening to Psalm 91 on an audio Bible. She spoke to me and was able to tell me my whole life story and said that God was waiting for me. And the third time, I had downloaded the YouVersion Bible app, and Psalm 91 popped up as the verse of the day. It was like God was speaking directly to me.

When I finally opened my Bible and read the psalm, the words pierced my heart: "He will save you from the fowler's snare and from the deadly pestilence. He will cover you with his feathers, and under his wings you will find refuge" (Ps. 91:3–4, NIV). Suddenly, I realized this was exactly what I had been searching for. I had been trying to carry fear and control everything on my own, but God was offering me His protection, His covering, His peace.

That night, I knelt and surrendered my life to Jesus. I told Him I couldn't do it on my own anymore. I asked Him to be my refuge, my Savior, and my strength. From that moment on, something changed. The fear that once consumed me began to break. I felt safe for the first time, not because my circumstances were perfect but because I knew I was in His hands.

Seeing Psalm 91 three times wasn't a coincidence. It was God's invitation. And I can say with all my heart now: When you run to Him, you really do find refuge.

CHAPTER 22

THE NARROW ROAD TO LIFE

Abundant (adjective)
: existing or occurring in large amounts
: amply supplied

IMAGINE STANDING AT a fork in the road. One path is wide, crowded, and full of noise. The other is narrow, hidden, and few even notice it's there. Jesus said it this way:

> You can enter God's Kingdom only through the narrow gate. The highway to hell is broad, and its gate is wide for the many who choose that way. But the gateway to life is very narrow and the road is difficult, and only a few ever find it.
>
> —MATTHEW 7:13–14

When He said those words, He wasn't giving us a motivational pep talk. He was drawing a line in the sand: two roads, two ways of life. And the choice isn't between religious people and sinners. It's between beggars and believers.

Beggars take the wide road. Believers take the narrow one. And friend, everything you've read in this book has been leading you right here. *This* is the road you've been looking for!

Let's be honest. Deep down, every single one of us has been

searching for life. Not just survival. Not just existing—*life*. The kind of life Jesus promised in John 10:10 (NKJV): "I have come that they may have life, and that they may have it more abundantly."

Abundant life isn't just a churchy phrase. It looks like peace that steadies you when the diagnosis comes back. It's the unexpected check that shows up the same week your hours got cut. It's a relationship you thought was dead being restored. That's abundance—not just surviving but seeing God show up in ways you could never engineer yourself.

Abundance *is* prosperity. But prosperity doesn't just mean money. Money is included in prosperity, but there is *so much* more to it than that. Prosperity means thriving, and that's what the narrow road delivers.

God is the provider. That means love, joy, and patience, sure. But it also means financial provision. The problem here is, our *provision* will always be attached to *His* vision, not ours. When we focus on ourselves, we may experience lack because we are focusing on a vision for our lives that didn't come from God. When we focus on Him and what He wants to do through us, there will *always* be enough provision to get it done. And there will be *more* than enough so that you can be a blessing to those around you as well! Remember, the hose always gets wet!

My friend, the narrow road is where the life you've dreamed about having with God turns into reality. Sadly, most people never find it. The wide road is packed with people chasing happiness, fulfillment, peace, purpose, and so on—all good things, but they're chasing them in the wrong way.

That's why Jesus said that few ever find it. Not because God is stingy. Not because it's hidden like some heavenly Easter egg. It's because the majority are still trying to find abundant life apart from the only One who *is* life.

The narrow road is different. The narrow road isn't about chasing. It's about trusting. It's about walking step-by-step. Not with desperation but with gratitude. And here's the twist that changes everything: Every single step you take on this narrow road is powered by two words. (You already know, don't you?) *Thank You!*

Think about how you walk. One foot in front of the other, steady rhythm, step after step. That's what the narrow road is like. But instead of physical steps with your feet, it's gratitude. One thank You after another.

Thank You, Father, for loving me when I was unlovable. Step.

Thank You for providing when I can't see a way out. Step.

That's the rhythm. Gratitude moves you forward.

Every thank You is a step forward. But a fear-filled *please* can trip you up. Why? Because *please* assumes you might not ever receive it. Faith says you already have it, so gratitude keeps your eyes locked on the provider.

Now, don't hear what I'm not saying. Not every *please* is wrong. Scripture shows us that petition has its place. The difference is this: A fear-driven *please* keeps you staring at your lack, but a faith-filled *please* still trusts God's promise and ends with thank You.

There's nothing wrong with asking God for what you need, but if asking becomes begging, you'll stay focused on your need instead of His supply. *Please* shifts the focus back to you without you even realizing it! Instead of being faith focused on what you *know* is coming in God's appropriate timing, you're just continuing to live in fear as you stare at your "lack of" now.

Paul even shows us this balance: "Do not be anxious about anything, but in every situation, by prayer and petition, with thanksgiving, present your requests to God" (Phil. 4:6, NIV). See it? Petition and gratitude are meant to work together. You can ask, but make sure your asking is wrapped in thanksgiving, not fear.

Beggars plead for scraps. Believers say thank You for the feast already prepared. And as you learn to walk like this, something wild happens. You realize the narrow road isn't hard in the way religion told you it would be. It's not miserable, restrictive, or joyless. It's full of freedom. It's full of peace. It's the life you've been looking for all along.

Let's zoom in.

The Wide Road (Beggars)	The Narrow Road (Believers)
Built on fear	Built on faith
Fueled by scarcity	Fueled by gratitude
Defined by begging God to "please, maybe, hopefully" show up	Defined by confidence in Jesus' finished work
Focused on what I don't have	Focused on who He is and what He's already done
Always searching, never finding	Always receiving, always overflowing
The wide road is easy to walk because it matches our flesh. It's natural to complain, natural to doubt. It's natural to crave control. But the problem is, it leads to death—death of joy, death of peace, and ultimately death of intimacy with God.	The narrow road is harder, not because it's complicated but because it requires surrender. It requires letting go of self, counting the cost. It requires trusting God more than you trust yourself. But the destination? *Life*. And not just someday-in-heaven life. Right here. Right now.

Now let's take this one level deeper. Walking the narrow road isn't just about how you pray. It's about how you live. And that's where the difference between having a castle mindset and kingdom mindset comes in.

The castle mindset (me-focused)—The castle mindset says, "This is my life, my time, my money, my plans, my dreams." It builds walls, digs moats, and spends all its energy protecting me, mine, and myself. The castle mindset lives on the wide road. Why? Because it's fueled by fear—fear of not having enough. Fear of being hurt. Fear of losing control. And fear will always turn you inward.

The kingdom mindset (God-focused)—The kingdom mindset flips the script. It says, "This is God's life, God's time, God's resources, God's plans, God's kingdom." Instead of protecting self, it pursues service. Instead of building walls, it opens doors. Instead of fear, it's fueled by faith. The kingdom mindset lives on the narrow road because it's all about God. His heart. His mission. His glory.

And here's the crazy thing: When you stop building your castle and start seeking His kingdom, you actually find what you were looking for in the first place.

That makes sense to you, doesn't it?

If thank You is every step we take on the narrow road, and thank You puts us in the presence of God, that is *exactly* where everything we could ever want or need is going to be found! "But seek first his kingdom and his righteousness, and all these things will be given to you as well" (Matt. 6:33, NIV). That's not just a verse for a refrigerator magnet. That's the narrow road in one sentence.

When we make the *choice* to say, "I'm not going to build my castle today. God, what can I do today to build Your kingdom?" what we are doing is releasing control! We are letting go of our lives and trusting that God can do more with us today than we ever could.

And since I'm not the one trying to make things happen anymore, now God can provide for me because I finally got out of His way!

It was shortly after I figured this out that Matthew 6:33 became my favorite verse in the Bible. I call it the secret to life. Because that's *exactly* what it is! The secret to the *abundant* life: Seek His kingdom, not my castle. Everything else will be taken care of for me.

Wow. I never get tired of that!

For some the beggar versus believer language might feel too black and white. But hear me: This isn't about perfection; it's about direction. Even believers still wrestle with beggar moments. The difference is that now we know where to turn.

Like Paul said in Philippians 4:6, we bring our petitions with thanksgiving. Like Jesus promised in John 10:10, we trust Him for a more abundant life. And when that shift happens, the change isn't just theological; it shows up in real life. A fearful "Please?" becomes a confident "Thank You!" A closed fist turns into an open hand. A chain falls off, and freedom begins.

So I think it's pretty safe to say that this leads us to only one question: Which road are *you* on? Do you know already how to find out? It's simple. Ask yourself these three questions—the same ones we've been unpacking all along:

1. **Am I a beggar or a believer?** Do I pray with *please* or *thank You*? Do I walk in fear or in faith?

2. **Who do I say Jesus is?** Is He just a distant figure, or is He the living God I trust daily?

3. **Who needs to be healed today?** Am I focused on my castle, or am I carrying the kingdom to others?

The answers *will* tell you which road your feet are on. Jesus said only a few find this road—and He's right. Most will keep chasing what they'll never catch. Most will keep begging when the banquet's already been set. But you don't have to be like most people. You've seen the truth. You've heard it. You've tasted it. And now you get to live it.

The narrow road isn't for the elite. It's for the surrendered. It's for the ones willing to trade *please* for *thank You*, fear for faith, castle for kingdom.

To access more content from Kelly K, scan the QR code or visit KellyKBooks.com/believer/ch22.

JON WHITE

In 2022 I got COVID and had continual breathing problems. I was misdiagnosed with pneumonia three times. In January 2024, the medical staff finally started checking for something else because pneumonia was not it. In February I was diagnosed with pulmonary fibrosis and instantly pulled out of work and disabled. I was now on oxygen. Four days later I was sent to the hospital with extremely low oxygen. I was in and out of the hospital three times for low oxygen.

On Saturday, March 30, 2024, I was airlifted to Vanderbilt Hospital. Over the next six days, I was put through several tests to see whether I was a candidate for a double lung transplant. Now, through most of this process, my walk with God was practically nonexistent—until I started the process for my transplant. I started begging God to save me from death. I didn't want to die. I wanted to be here for my kids and grandkids.

During the week of testing, I began to tell God that I wanted His will to be done in my life. I stopped begging and began to believe that whatever happens is God's will. On Friday, April 5, I was approved for a double lung transplant, and on April 7 the surgery took place. A couple of months after the surgery, my doctor asked me whether I knew just how sick I really was. When I landed at Vanderbilt, I had been given only seven to fourteen days to live.

Over this last year and a half, my walk with God has been "thank You" for each and every day. God's guidance is what drives me today. God has opened the opportunity to be more involved in church, and I have accepted that role. Every time I take a deep breath, I *thank God* for each and every one. Glory!

CHAPTER 23

LIVE WITH GREAT EXPECTATION

Expectation (noun)

: a strong belief that something will happen or be the case in the future[1]

: a belief that someone will or should achieve something[2]

PETER WROTE, "ALL praise to God, the Father of our Lord Jesus Christ. It is by his great mercy that we have been born again, because God raised Jesus Christ from the dead. Now we live *with great expectation*" (1 Pet. 1:3). Expectation aimed at timing breeds disappointment. Expectation aimed at Jesus breeds life.

We're going somewhere here, but first, I hope now you can see that every single person on earth is living up to, or down to, their own revelation of the freedom Jesus bought for them.

Do you get it? Those walking on the narrow road understand exactly how free they are—because they are constantly staring at the One who set them free! They understand that the law isn't a list of rules; it's a mirror to show you that you're dirty. Jesus is the One who washed you clean!

Those of us walking on the narrow road understand that to "fix" the sin in our lives, there is nothing *we* can do at all! We just keep looking to the Father so He can keep doing what He promised He would: change us from the inside out. We kill the root of rebellion by shifting our focus, and the fruit will wither on its own! But those on the wide path will never fully see their freedom because they can't stop focusing on their own chains.

However, there is one more key piece of information you're going to need to keep you walking on this narrow path. You need to understand *expectation*. In 1 Peter 1:3–4, we read,

> All praise to God, the Father of our Lord Jesus Christ. It is by his great mercy that we have been born again, because God raised Jesus Christ from the dead. Now we live with great expectation, and we have a priceless inheritance—an inheritance that is kept in heaven for you, pure and undefiled, beyond the reach of change and decay.

What Peter is telling us here is that because of the finished works of Jesus on the cross (*sōzō*), *now we* get to live with *great* expectation. We get to expect miracles and healing in our lives *and* the lives of others! We get to expect breakthroughs and deliverance from the things keeping us in sin! We get to expect that all our needs will be met according to His riches and glory!

Is this getting you excited? It should be! But there is a flip side. While *yes*, we need to live with great expectations, we also need to know how to *aim* our expectations.

Let me show you what I mean. When you and I talk about our expectations—for ourselves, another person, a situation, whatever—we normally expect *what* we want to happen, *when* we want it to happen, and *how* we want it to happen. Sounds accurate so far?

But when it comes to God? Yeah, no. It doesn't work like that. It *can't* work like that. You understand *why*, right?

> "My thoughts are nothing like your thoughts," says the Lord. "And my ways are far beyond anything you could imagine. For just as the heavens are higher than the

> earth, so my ways are higher than your ways and my thoughts higher than your thoughts."
>
> —Isaiah 55:8–9

The reason it *can't* work like our normal expectations is that God isn't like us! His plan goes beyond ours. He sees outside of us. He knows how each prayer request being fulfilled or denied will impact others decades after we pray it. He knows what you and I could never know: *tomorrow*.

This is also why all He truly asks us to do is trust Him. Trust that He sees beyond us and He knows better than us. Trust that *His plan is better*! Because it always is. So when Peter said, "Now we live with great expectation," he did not *at all* mean expectations about the where, when, and how.

We usually think in terms of the "who, what, when, where, and why." But when it comes to our expectations with God, only two things matter: *who* and *why*. That is the key. *Who* is the One doing the work. *Why* is the reason He does it—because He loves us and already paid for it. If you try to hang your faith on the other three (when, where, and what), you're setting yourself up for disappointment. And disappointment leads to a lack of trust. And a lack of trust leads to wandering eyes—a loss of focus on Him.

You see, again, when you live on the narrow road, these two words are the steps you take to move forward: "Thank You." That's gratitude. Before you receive something, say, "Thank You." That puts you in a state of expectation. It has to. You just said thank You in faith! That means you actually *believe* it's coming!

If I pray, "Thank You, Father, that my spouse's back *is* healed, in Jesus' name!" my expectation is, "God, *You* are the One healing them! However and whenever You do it is totally up to *You*! I'm just saying thank You in advance!"

The truth is, healing can come in a lot of different ways. God's ways are not our ways! God can heal in a moment. He can heal through doctors. He can finish the healing in eternity. Gratitude says, "Father, You are the healer. I trust Your wisdom and timing." That keeps my eyes on *who*, not my calendar.

Sometimes healing looks like years of treatment. Sometimes breakthrough feels painful. Sometimes provision shows up as an idea, not a check in the mail. And if you were expecting the answer to the prayer in the time frame *you* wanted, the way *you* wanted, how *you* wanted it to happen, your life will be *full* of disappointment. You will lose your trust in God and His Word, and eventually you will be right back on the wide road, begging God again, because you never saw what *you* wanted to see.

Ouch. I know that stings a little. It needs to.

So what do you do in that moment when the prayer isn't answered the way you wanted and disappointment starts to creep in? Here's the shift:

1. Pause. Stop replaying the when, where, or how in your mind.

2. Say, "Thank You," out loud. Even if your feelings don't line up, open your mouth and thank God for already being at work.

3. Name the *who*. Remind yourself, "Father, You are the One who heals, provides, and delivers. It's not on me; it's on You."

4. Anchor in the *why*. Whisper, "I gave You my life. I trust Your plan over mine."

That's how you drag your eyes off disappointment and lock them back on Jesus in real time. We need to decide, right now, "I will not put unrealistic expectations on our Father. I will trust Him instead!" When we focus *only* on the *who* and *why*, we will *never* be disappointed!

How? I'll show you!

When my expectation is simply, "God, I know You are the One who is going to make this happen. I trust You!" my focus stays on Him. Not my calendar. Not my watch. Not my idea of how I want God to work. If it happens today, "Sweet! Thank You, Father! That was fast!" If it doesn't, "No problem, Father. I trust that Your timing is *perfect*!" We need to have all the expectation in the world on *who*, and none on when, where, and what.

To help you continue the journey down the narrow path, the best way I can explain it is like this: Expect *nothing* and *everything* at the same time! You will *never* be disappointed! Does that make sense?

Hold expectation in two ways at once: "By faith, it's mine now; by trust, I'm content with His timing." That's how you stay unshaken.

I'm expecting that the moment I pray, my miracle belongs to me right that second. And with the same breath, since I *trust* Him, I don't *need* it to show up while I'm on earth at all. I am willing to wait 'til heaven. Why?

Exactly. *Why!*

Our expectation is on *who* and *why*. Why can I have expectations at all? Because I gave up my life, and now Jesus lives *through* me. Remember? No one in the cemetery is worried about when or how their bills are going to get paid. They are dead! And so are we. That is the *why*. I gave up my life, my plans, my agenda, my wants, my desires, my opinions, my *everything*!

So whether the answer to my request shows up on earth or in heaven, it makes no difference to me. My life is *not* my own. Each day, each word, each choice, each action is simply God living through me. How could I *ever* be disappointed with a life like *that*?

Here's the bottom line: If you've given your life to Christ, your life is not your own anymore. That means no wasted days, no wasted pain, no wasted storms. God is using all of it to shape you. James could say, "I count it all joy," because he trusted two things: *who* was in control and *why* he was still breathing. That's it. And that's your call too.

When it's a good day, say thank You. When it's a hard day,

still say thank You. Either way, your expectation stays fixed on the One who never fails. That is what it really means to walk the narrow road—not just heading toward heaven one day but letting heaven live through you today.

Friend, this is it. This is the road. The narrow road to life is not just the path to heaven. It's the path of heaven coming alive in you right now. So just to remove any confusion whatsoever, here is how to walk the narrow road practically. You've heard the truth. Now it's time to practice it. Here are three ways to put feet on this message starting today:

1. Morning gratitude

Before your feet hit the floor, whisper three simple thank-yous:

- "Thank You, Father, for another day. I trust *You* and *Your* timing.."
- "Thank You, Jesus, that You've already forgiven me."
- "Thank You, Holy Spirit, for guiding me today."

That's it. Three thank-yous. Start there.

2. A kingdom-first checklist

Now, as many times as you can, but at least once during your day, stop and ask,

- "Am I building my castle right now, or God's kingdom?"
- "Whose name am I trying to make bigger: mine or His?"
- "Is fear or faith driving this choice?"
- "Where is my expectation aimed?"

Write these questions on a sticky note or on your phone. Let them guide your daily decisions.

3. A seven-day "thank You" prayer experiment

For one week, shift your language. Every time you're tempted to pray, "Please, God," reframe it as, "Thank You, Father, that You are already working on this."

Keep a small journal of what happens. You'll start to see how gratitude changes not just your words but your faith, your peace, and even your outlook on life.

Now that you *know* you are a believer and not a beggar, you've got the tools in your hands! Gratitude, a kingdom-first focus, and a new way to pray. That's how you walk the narrow road with expectation that never disappoints.

Stay in it. Stay sharp. Stay surrendered.

To access more content from Kelly K, scan the QR code or visit KellyKBooks.com/believer/ch23.

ANONYMOUS

Out of the blue one day, my teenage son came to me and shared that he had sleep paralysis: He sees things that are not really there. He hears things that are not there, and things attack him in his sleep.

I'm a pretty attentive parent, but I had no idea. How long had this been going on? How could I not see it? Over the course of a year and a half or so—through multiple doctors' appointments and counseling visits—my son began to open up a little more and share. He said that he didn't really believe in God—he wasn't sure whether he ever had. I felt so crushed, defeated, worried, and terrified.

With everything going on in the world today, I wanted to help my son, of course, but I was also scared to put him in the hands of some

of the "caregivers" in the medical and therapeutic professions, as well as in schools. I was begging God to help me. "God, please help him get rest; please protect my son. God, please, whatever is attacking him or making him ill, cast it out."

I had stumbled across one of Kelly K's videos on TikTok before this all started, and I joined the daily Bible studies in the mornings. Doing *daily church* together really helped me get through this time. It truly changed how I pray. Kelly taught us repeatedly that God won't do what He's already done, and He already sent His Son, Jesus, to die on the cross to save us, heal us, and deliver us. That includes my son, and that includes me. I started praying, "Thank You, God, that You love my son more than I could, even though I can't fathom that. Thank You, Father, for healing him, for giving him sleep, for giving him peace. Thank You for giving me authority over my house to cast out any spirits that are trying to attack my family."

As we went through this process with doctors, tests, scans, and counselors, things were slowly getting a little better, but as soon as I shifted to praying with thanks and believing the promises of God, my anxieties dropped dramatically. I don't know how I could've functioned if I had tried to continue down the begging path.

My son hasn't seen or heard anything that is not really there in quite some time. I believe this was a spiritual attack against my family. We have prayed together, and I continue to pray in belief and thanks for all God has done for us. The healing was not instantaneous, but it was paid for two-thousand-plus years ago on the cross, and I will continue to thank Him for it.

My son still occasionally goes to a Christian counselor to talk through the things that might be bothering him (he is a teenager, after all). But he does believe in God, and he prays and talks to God.

I thank God for this church family and for Pastor Kelly helping us get through this scary time. I am so glad I learned the lesson that I should not beg—there was no power in that. Now I pray with the belief of what He's already done for me, and I'm so thankful.

CHAPTER 24

BENNIE AND MELISSA

Testimony (noun)

: firsthand authentication of a fact

: a public profession of religious experience

OK, NOW IT'S time to make this personal. Let me tell you a story about my friends Bennie and Melissa. This isn't theory. This isn't a sermon illustration. This is real life.

What happened with Bennie and Melissa was no sitcom. It was raw, painful, and miraculous, and it will show you exactly how living with expectation as a believer and not a beggar changes everything.

I have been in full-time ministry for over ten years. In this last decade, God has changed, reshaped, repurposed, and moved this ministry in ways I never could have seen coming! It has been a wild ride, to say the least!

About three years ago, God told me to start doing a *live* Bible study every morning. At first I didn't want to. I mean, come on, that's way too risky, right? Too unpredictable. But I obeyed. And from day one, God blew the doors open. Thousands joined, people got saved, and the community kept growing.

I couldn't do it alone. It was getting to be too much. One person trying to keep up with thousands? Ha! Yeah, I was struggling. So we added moderators. (I absolutely *love* my moderators!) These are extremely faithful people who serve this ministry every single day.

Two of them are Bennie and Melissa. And their story is one you need to hear.

In 2009 Melissa gave her life to Jesus. But like so many of us, she was saved, yet she never learned to stay in His Word and walk in daily relationship, trusting Him. She loved God. But she was still trying to manage life on her own. She added Him to her plans instead of surrendering to His.

Melissa spent years begging God. Begging for a baby. Begging for a family. Begging for her prayers to finally be answered. She had walked through more pain than most could imagine. An abusive marriage. A tubal pregnancy that ruptured and ended with emergency surgery. Years on fertility drugs that never worked. A divorce. Disappointment after disappointment.

Her heart was crushed, and her prayers became desperate. "God, *please* make me a mom!" "God, *please* fix this!" "God, *please* give me what I've been asking for!" Sounds familiar? She didn't realize it at the time, but Melissa was living like a beggar, not a believer.

In 2017 she met Bennie. They became best friends, started dating, and by 2020 they were engaged. Both of them longed to be parents. Both had faced heartbreak and church hurt. And both still thought the goal was to chase their dream and hope God blessed it. But God had a better plan.

In November 2023 Bennie stumbled across one of my videos online and sent it to Melissa. By the beginning of 2024, they were tuning in daily to our online live Bible study. That's when the shift happened. Instead of begging God, they started *thanking* Him—thanking Him for each other. Thanking Him for loving them when they felt unworthy. Thanking Him for things they couldn't even see yet but trusted He would provide.

That's faith! Hebrews 11:1 says, "Faith shows the reality of what we hope for; it is the evidence of things we cannot see." They stopped pleading like beggars and started praising like believers.

And guess what? *Everything* began to change: their marriage, their relationships, their peace, their joy. By April 2024 they were in the Word every single day. By August they fasted for the very first time with our Bible study family. And the very same day—August 1, 2024—they got the call from their adoption agency: "Your profile is now live. Expectant mothers can start seeing your story."

That wasn't a coincidence. That was God moving.

Now, at this point Melissa would want me to tell you, "Be careful what you pray for when using a faith-fueled thank You!" In November they prayed, "Father, thank You for removing anything in our lives that pushes us away from You or keeps us from growing in You." And in her own words: "Watch out—He will do it!" Because He did.

God started stripping things away—not to punish them but to prepare them. In December they were presented with the opportunity to adopt a baby girl in California with special needs. In the past, they would have said no instantly. But instead, they prayed.

Melissa's heart shifted in a way that shocked even her. She stopped praying, "Lord, give me this baby," and started praying, "Lord, let this mother keep her baby if that's Your will." That's kingdom over castle. That's putting God's heart above personal desire.

And guess what? A week later, the mom decided to keep her daughter.

Instead of being crushed, Bennie and Melissa celebrated. "Hallelujah! God's will is better!" That's when you know you've crossed from begging to believing.

If this were the only setback they had—eh, no big deal.. But it wasn't. They faced scams too. A woman reached out during a Bible study claiming she was pregnant and looking for adoptive parents. But what looked like hope soon turned to disappointment. Everyone told them it was fake. But they just wanted to believe it was real, so bad!

It wasn't.

But instead of bitterness, they chose love. They prayed for her, supported her, started a friendship, and even now still reach out when she calls. God brings people into our lives in the most insane ways sometimes! That's why our trust in *Him* is so vital—not in people, circumstances, or situations.

At this point for Bennie and Melissa, this wasn't about getting a child at all costs. It was about trusting God's timing, God's plan, and God's heart. And that's when the final test came.

In May 2025 Bennie and Melissa got a call. They had been chosen as finalists by an expecting mom! Can you even *begin* to imagine their excitement? It was down to them and one other family. Melissa wrote a prayer for the birth mom that wasn't, "God, please let her pick us." It was about God's will. About peace. About protection.

She sent it. The mom got it. And then came the call. The mom chose the other family.

Ouch. Just typing that out made my heart hurt.

Beggar Melissa would've been devastated. But believer Melissa? She said, "That's exactly what I prayed for—that she would have clarity." But deep down she also knew the story wasn't over.

Just two days later, Melissa was at a prayer gathering. God pressed her heart. She decided to *finally* let go completely. "Lord, I give You my desire to be a mom. If it's not Your plan, I don't want it. I trust You." That was the narrow road—not chasing her own dream anymore. Not begging for what *she* wanted but surrendering fully to God's perfect plan, whatever that may be. And the peace that came was overwhelming.

On Friday, May 9, 2025, the phone rang again. It was the adoption agency.

The very same mom who had chosen the other family was in the hospital having an emergency C-section. The baby was coming a month early! That was apparently one month too soon for the family this mom had selected to adopt her baby. That family backed out.

And God? God had chosen Bennie and Melissa all along! At 10:28 a.m., a healthy baby boy was born. It was a Friday. Bennie and Melissa had to wait until Sunday to actually meet and hold their new baby son. And would you look at God—that Sunday was *Mother's Day*.

That's right! On Mother's Day, Melissa held her son for the first time. The next day, it was official. They were parents. Now *that* is a testimony!

Do you see it? This wasn't just an adoption story. This was the gospel in action. Melissa spent years as a beggar, pleading with God. But when she shifted to thanksgiving, she became a believer. She discovered that Jesus is more than the giver of gifts—He *is* the gift.

She learned that sometimes the one who needs healing is you: healing from disappointment, wrong thinking, and living like a beggar. And when the healing finally came, it wasn't just the child she longed for; it was peace, joy, and surrender.

Psalm 37:4 says, "Take delight in the Lord, and he will give you your heart's desires." That's exactly what happened.

So what about you? Have you decided yet? Are you a beggar or a believer? Are you walking the wide road or the narrow one? Is your focus still on you or on the Father? The choice is yours. But don't miss this moment.

Bartimaeus almost did. Don't let that be your story.

To access more content from Kelly K, scan the QR code or visit KellyKBooks.com/believer/ch24.

MELISSA OUZTS

I was saved in 2009 but never had a relationship and prayer life with God like I do today.

This all changed the day my husband forwarded me a TikTok video of Kelly. I knew my husband was a believer, but neither of us read our Bibles or sent messages with scriptures in them! So this was a *wow*

moment for me! Not only was I surprised my husband sent this to me, but when I opened the video, I *never* expected this guy to begin preaching!

I watched the entire video and immediately messaged my husband and said, "That was a surprise." Come to find out, my husband had been watching his videos for weeks! After that day, my husband and I began joining Kelly's live Bible studies. I learned so much more about God and becoming a believer and not a beggar. When I was initially saved, I was always begging God in my prayers and daily life. I was only in the Word when I went to church once a week, and maybe for a Bible study. Oh, son, have I changed!

I got it. God sent His one and only Son to die for us so that our sins would be forgiven. God knows all the sins we have done and all the sins we will do, and they are already forgiven. We only need to repent and *give it to God*! When explained by Kelly, it was like a light bulb flipped on! I was begging God to be forgiven over and over again like an annoying child, but it was because I didn't understand and hadn't truly forgiven myself. I needed to *give everything to God*. I began my life as a believer, as *God has already won*!

My life and relationship with God are incredible! I want to be in His Word as much as possible, and definitely more than once a week. I would go crazy if I couldn't get in His Word daily now! The feeling of freedom and no stress after giving my entire life to Him is the best feeling *ever*. I am a believer and a doer of His Word!

My prayer life has completely changed. Instead of begging God for things, I thank Him! I am a believer and trust in His Word and His timing. My marriage has become strong now that we have both placed God first and our marriage second in our lives. He makes our marriage stronger every day, and I thank God for this daily!

I cannot even imagine the emotional roller coaster that the adoption process would have been for us if we hadn't become believers and doers. We thank God daily for our adoption journey, for strengthening us during difficult times, and for being with us at all times throughout our adoption process.

I could write on and on about how much my life has changed from that one video my husband forwarded me that one day! Thank you, Kelly, for sharing His Word with us! We thank God for placing you in our lives and pray for you and your family daily!

CHAPTER 25

LAST CHANCE

Moment (noun)

: a minute portion or point of time—instant

: a comparatively brief period of time

ALL RIGHT, MY friend, we did it. We've made it to the end of the book. But don't miss this: What you're about to read could change everything. Along the way, I haven't just challenged your thoughts. I've asked you to confront your life. Now, before we put a bow on this and wrap it up, let's rewind one last time.

Remember blind Bartimaeus? The beggar sitting on the side of the road when Jesus came passing by? Of course you do. Here's something wild that most people miss: That was the last miracle in the Book of Mark that Jesus performed before the cross. The very last one. Think about *that* for a minute.

The next time He stepped into Jerusalem, He wasn't stopping to heal blind men anymore. He was riding a donkey, headed toward betrayal, beating, and the brutal crucifixion that would pay for the sins of the world. So when Bartimaeus cried out, "Jesus, Son of David, have mercy on me!" that was it. His last shot. His one chance. His only moment.

And the crowd? They told him to shut up. To sit down. To stop calling out. But Bartimaeus didn't listen. He cried out louder. And because he refused to be silenced, Jesus stopped, called him over, and healed him. If Bartimaeus had listened to the crowd, he would have stayed blind forever.

What I'm trying to say is—*don't miss your moment*!

Here's the sobering truth: There comes a point for every single one of us when it's too late to call on Jesus. We don't like to think about that. We'd rather believe we have endless time. But the Bible makes it clear: "Today is the day of salvation" (2 Cor. 6:2). Not tomorrow. Not someday. Not when life slows down.

Today. Right now.

Bartimaeus didn't know Jesus was about to give up His life. He didn't know this was his last shot. He only knew the healer was near—and that was enough to cry out with everything he had.

Friend, you and I don't know how much time we've got left either. Life is fragile. Time is short. And eternity is forever. Think about it. Bartimaeus didn't know that moment was his last shot before the cross. And neither do we.

One day, each of us will stand before Jesus, not as the healer passing by on the road but as the judge seated on the throne. Hebrews 9:27 says, "Each person is destined to die once and after that comes judgment." That means there is no second chance after the last breath. No rewinds. No bargaining. No crowd to shout over. Just you, standing before the King.

Bartimaeus's desperation on the roadside is a picture of the desperation every soul will feel in that moment. The difference is that by then it will be too late to cry out. That's why the Bible keeps saying today is the day of salvation.

For my lifelong Christian readers, don't miss this: Bartimaeus didn't assume he had another day, another sermon, another chance. He cried out immediately. Right away. That urgency is how we're called to live. Every prayer, every thank You, every act of faith is not practice for someday—it's preparation for eternity.

That's why you have to know what you believe. You have to know *who* you believe in. And you have to know who you are now because of what you believe. This whole book has been leading to this moment. Let's look back at what we've learned.

Beggars plead like God hasn't spoken. *Believers* thank Him because the cross already finished it. (John 19:30: "It is finished!")

Beggars chase blessings. *Believers* chase Jesus—and the blessings follow. (Matthew 6:33: "Seek the Kingdom of God above all else, and live righteously, and he will give you everything you need.")

Beggars focus on their castle: their wants, their comfort, their everything. *Believers* live for the kingdom: God's will, God's glory, God's people.

Beggars crumble in rebellion when their eyes shift from God to themselves. *Believers* stand firm in surrender, keeping their gaze locked on the Father. (Hebrews 12:2: "We do this by keeping our eyes on Jesus, the champion who initiates and perfects our faith.")

Beggars wait for life to change before they praise. *Believers* praise in the waiting and watch life transform. (Philippians 4:6–7: "Don't worry about anything; instead, pray about everything. Tell God what you need, and thank him for all he has done. Then you will experience God's peace.")

It's the same lesson Bartimaeus lived. The crowd wanted him to stay in beggar mode: quiet, small, and ignored. But Bartimaeus believed. He cried out. He refused to beg man for attention and instead believed Jesus for a miracle.

Jesus said, "But the gateway to life is very narrow and the road is difficult, and only a few ever find it" (Matt. 7:14). Most people settle for the wide road. The wide road is full of beggars: people chasing the next thing, pleading for scraps, living in survival mode, with eyes locked on self. It's easy, sure. It's comfortable, I guess. But it's also crowded, and it leads to destruction.

But the narrow road? That's where life is. Real life. Abundant life. The life you've been craving but could never quite grab on to.

And how do you walk it? Step after step of gratitude. One thank You in front of another. Instead of, "Please, God, give me peace," it's, "Thank You, Father, that You are my peace." Rather than saying, "Please, God, heal me," it's, "Thank You, Jesus, that by Your wounds I am healed." In place of, "Please, God, provide," it's, "Thank You, Lord, that You are my provider."

That's the narrow road.

Remember, your life isn't meant to be a cup you clutch, hoping it gets filled once in a while. You're a hose made to stay connected to the source so that His love keeps flowing through you to others. That's why Paul could say, "And this same God who takes care of me will supply all your needs from his glorious riches, which have been given to us in Christ Jesus" (Phil. 4:19).

Needs aren't the problem—focus is. If you're focused on your castle, you'll always feel empty. If you're focused on the kingdom, you'll always overflow.

A castle mindset is small. It's you building walls around yourself. The kingdom mindset tears those walls down and asks, "How can my life build His kingdom?" Melissa's story in the previous chapter proved it. For decades she begged God from a castle mindset. But when she surrendered to the kingdom, when she stopped begging and started thanking, everything shifted. Her miracle came—not on her timeline but on God's perfect schedule.

So here you are. The end of this book. The edge of decision. Your Bartimaeus moment.

Will you listen to the crowd and stay seated in the dirt of your old life? Or will you cry out louder, reach for Jesus, and step onto the narrow road? Because make no mistake, my friend—this isn't just the last chapter of a book. This is the last call out of a beggar life.

You can't just go back to living the way you did before. It's impossible. You know too much now. And that's a good thing! Your old way of praying, believing, trusting, *living* will never be the same again. It can't be! And not because of my words. (Who am I?) It's because now you will have the Holy Spirit reminding you of these things every single day! And the truth is, He wants you to live as a believer and not a beggar even more than you do!

The wide road is crowded. The narrow road is waiting. Which one are you stepping onto?

Let's seal it with this prayer. If you're ready to move from beggar to believer, pray this out loud:

> *Father, thank You for loving me. Thank You for saving me. Thank You that I don't have to beg for what You've already given me access to through Jesus. Today, I choose to step onto the narrow road. I fix my eyes on You. I lay down my castle and live for Your kingdom. I choose to be a hose, not a cup—to let Your love, power, and provision flow through me to others. I trust You. I thank You. And I will walk every step of my life with thanksgiving on my lips. In Jesus' name, amen.*

My friend, the same Jesus who stopped for Bartimaeus is walking by you right now. Don't let Him pass. Cry out. Stand up. Take off your jacket and *run*!

Step onto the narrow road. And watch your beggar life transform into a believer's testimony. Because the truth is, you didn't just get to the end of a book.

You just stepped into the beginning of a brand-new life.

To access more content from Kelly K, scan the QR code or visit KellyKBooks.com/believer/ch25.

BRANDY MANGUM

There was a season in my life when my prayers for my son felt desperate. I watched him walking down a path filled with bad influences, loneliness, depression, and drinking, and as a mother it broke my heart. My prayers were full of pleading and begging, asking God to "please do something." It felt like I was praying from a place of fear instead of faith because I was scared and full of anxiety.

But then Kelly started teaching about praying like a believer. In this teaching I learned that I didn't need to pray as if God wasn't listening, but to pray with the confidence and trust that He already had a plan for my son's life and God loved my son even more than I did. My prayers shifted. I went from begging to believing. Instead of only asking, I began to thank God in advance for what He was going to do. I thanked Him for surrounding my son with the right people, for pulling him out of depression, for giving him joy again, and even for bringing a godly, positive voice into his life. And oh, son! God worked on me and through me in such a mighty way from that moment forward.

And I am thankful that today I can say—God answered. My son has come out of that dark place. He's no longer bound by loneliness and destructive choices. God placed a young woman in his life who speaks positivity, hope, and encouragement into him. The very things I thanked God for before—I can see them now unfolding before my eyes. God is *so* good. You have no idea how it feels to finally see my son get his joy back, how it feels to see him smiling and laughing again!

This testimony is not just about my son's turnaround; it's about the faithfulness of God and the power of believing prayer. When I stopped praying out of fear and anxiety and started praying with bold faith and thanking Him for things I could not see yet, peace filled my heart. And God showed me that He had been working all along.

Thank you, Kelly, for teaching me how to turn my prayer life upside down and view it in a different way, to see God in a different way, and to walk in His promises and claim them from a heart filled with thanks. Yes and amen, amen, amen!

CONCLUSION

KEEP WALKING

If you've made it here, I want to tell you something straight up: I'm proud of you. You didn't just skim words on a page. You leaned in. You wrestled. You let the Holy Spirit stir something inside you. You finished what you started.

But this isn't the end. It's not even close.

The moment Bartimaeus cried out wasn't the end of his story; it was the beginning. He got up, threw his beggar's cloak aside, and followed Jesus down the road. That's the invitation in front of you right now.

Don't shelve this book and slip back into "normal." There's no normal anymore. You've seen too much. You know too much. And you've tasted something real. So keep walking. Step after step. Day after day. Gratitude on your lips. Faith in your heart. Eyes locked on Jesus.

And if you ever doubt, ever stumble, ever feel like slipping back into beggar mode, remember this: The same Jesus who stopped for Bartimaeus is still walking with you today.

This is your new beginning. Walk it out.

Think about *that* for a minute!

—Kelly K

A PERSONAL INVITATION FROM THE AUTHOR

God loves you deeply. His Word is filled with promises that reveal His desire to bring healing, hope, and abundant life to every area of your being: body, mind, and spirit. More than anything, He wants a personal relationship with you through His Son, Jesus Christ.

If you've never invited Jesus into your life, you can do so right now. It's not about religion; it's about a relationship with the One who knows you completely and loves you unconditionally. If you're ready to take that step, simply pray this prayer with a sincere heart:

> *Lord Jesus, I want to know You as my Savior and Lord. I confess and believe that You are the Son of God and that You died for my sins. I believe that You rose from the dead and are alive today. Please forgive me for my sins. I invite You into my heart and my life. Make me new. Help me walk with You, grow in Your love, and live for You every day. In Jesus' name, amen.*

To hear me personally share about what it means to follow Christ, scan the QR code or visit KellyKBooks.com/believer/invitation.

If you just prayed that prayer, you've made the most important decision of your life. All of heaven rejoices with you, and so do I! You are now a child of God, and your journey with Him has just begun. Please reach out to my publisher at pray4me@charismamedia.com if you accepted Jesus today or if this book has encouraged or impacted your life in any way. We'd love to celebrate with you and send you free materials to help strengthen your faith. We look forward to hearing from you!

NOTES

Chapter 1

1. Larry Wachowski and Andy Wachowski, "*The Matrix*," The Internet Movie Script Database, accessed October 21, 2025, https://imsdb.com/scripts/Matrix,-The.html.

Chapter 2

1. *Cambridge Dictionary*, "same," accessed October 21, 2025, https://dictionary.cambridge.org/us/dictionary/english/same.
2. Encyclopedia.com, "Great," updated May 23, 2018, https://www.encyclopedia.com/places/britain-ireland-france-and-low-countries/british-and-irish-political-geography/great-0.
3. Encyclopedia.com, "Great."

Chapter 5

1. *Cambridge Dictionary*, "not see the wood for the trees," accessed October 22, 2025, https://dictionary.cambridge.org/dictionary/english/not-see-the-wood-for-the-trees.

Chapter 6

1. Encyclopedia.com, "Commission," updated May 14, 2018, https://www.encyclopedia.com/social-sciences-and-law/political-science-and-government/military-affairs-nonnaval/commission.
2. Encyclopedia.com, "Commission."
3. Blue Letter Bible, "*megas*," accessed October 27, 2025, https://www.blueletterbible.org/lexicon/g3173/kjv/tr/0-1/.

Chapter 7

1. Kelly Konya, "Moot Point: Definition and Examples," Grammarly, updated September 1, 2022, https://www.grammarly.com/blog/vocabulary/moot-point/.
2. Konya, "Moot Point."

Chapter 8

1. Dictionary.com, "catalyst," accessed October 27, 2025, https://www.dictionary.com/browse/catalyst.

Chapter 9

1. "Mercy Quotes," Jesuit Resource, accessed October 27, 2025, https://www.xavier.edu/jesuitresource/online-resources/quote-archive1/mercy-quotes.

Chapter 13

1. *Cambridge Dictionary*, "faith," accessed October 29, 2025, https://dictionary.cambridge.org/us/dictionary/english/faith.
2. *Merriam-Webster*, "reality," thesaurus entry, accessed October 29, 2025, https://www.merriam-webster.com/thesaurus/reality.
3. *Merriam-Webster*, "evidence," thesaurus entry, accessed October 29, 2025, https://www.merriam-webster.com/thesaurus/evidence.

Chapter 17

1. "Practicing Christian: Witness," YouVersion, accessed October 29, 2025, https://www.bible.com/events/49336798.
2. Dan Wood, "Redeeming Lost Time," Sermons by Logos, accessed October 29, 2025, https://sermons.logos.com/sermons/218499-redeeming-lost-time.

Chapter 18

1. "The Problem with Authority," Metris Leadership, accessed October 31, 2025, https://metrisleadership.com/the-problem-with-authority/.

Chapter 19

1. Mayo Clinic Staff, "Cataracts," Mayo Clinic, accessed October 31, 2025, https://www.mayoclinic.org/diseases-conditions/cataracts/symptoms-causes/syc-20353790, paraphrased.

Chapter 21

1. Dictionary.com, "hose," accessed October 31, 2025, https://www.dictionary.com/browse/hose.
2. Dictionary.com, "hose."

Chapter 23

1. Nife Oluyemi, "Expectations," Medium, February 3, 2017, https://nife.medium.com/expectations-2e8f16664e20.
2. Monique Kalmar, "Expectations…," Psychology Pathways, September 1, 2016, https://psychologypathways.com/expectations/.

ACKNOWLEDGMENTS

LINDSAY KOPP: THERE are no words that allow me to express my gratitude for you accurately! You are my best friend, my partner, my ride or die, my *everything*! Thank you for all the times you helped lift me up when the weight of writing this book was weighing me down. Thank you for believing in me and the call God placed on my life, even when so many didn't. Myself included! Thank you for keeping me grounded when I start to get carried away, but also thank you for encouraging me to dream bigger when my vision is too small! Thank you for being *you*! There is no comparison! I love you more and more each day, and I am honored to get to be your husband! I am forever yours—faithfully!

Kale Suedkamp: Bro! Where do I even begin? The friend and partner I never knew I wanted or needed! But God did! I am constantly thanking the Father for you! He put you in my life when I needed you most, and I am forever grateful! Thank you for all your hard work and the time you put in helping me write this book. It wouldn't be what it is without your input, suggestions, edits, and corrections. Thank you for always telling me the *truth* and not just what you think I want to hear. Even when you know I won't be happy, you give it to me straight! I value that in you more than you even know. Thank you for *all* you do for me, my family, my ministry, and most definitely for what you did with this book! I say we don't slow down now! This is only the beginning! I can't wait to see where God is going to lead us next! I'm stoked to be on this path with you!

Ryan Edberg, Luke Aadalen, Pastor Randy Henderson, moderators, and everyone who is a part of Kelly K Ministries: Thank you all for your radical generosity! You each bring something special and unique to our team, and this wouldn't be what it is without you! You serve and give your time, money, blood, sweat, and tears to make this ministry what it is, and I promise you that it doesn't go unnoticed. I thank God daily for each of you, and I pray that one day I am able to give back a blessing to you as great as you have given me! Let's keep going! From glory to glory! We are just getting started!

Moderators and faithful members of our live online Bible study: *We did it!* Thank you all so much! This book is a product of our time together! You guys helped me prepare and write this without ever knowing it. So much of the teaching in this book came out of our time together. I want you to know how grateful I am for you. Because I know you are all going to show up every morning hungry for God's Word, that has *forced* me (in the best way) to dive deeper into the Word myself and not to miss or skip my quiet time with the Father on days my flesh starts to get the best of me. My relationship with God has only grown and gotten stronger because of it! I had no idea how badly I needed you all in my life! I pray that this book is as much of a blessing to you as each of you has been to me! Thank you! I'll keep showing up every morning if you will!

Kelly K Ministry partners: How can I ever thank you enough? You guys have made a choice to sow into this ministry financially—not just once but on a regular, consistent basis. Wow! I'm not sure I can even properly explain to you how much of a blessing that is! I will never forget the days when our ministry lived from Sunday to Sunday, only making money if I had a church to speak in that week. Or the days when we didn't always know how we were going to keep the lights on, or how we were going to get to the next event, when Harlan and Susan Robertson were pretty much single-handedly keeping this ministry going with their monthly donation (and they're still here! I love you guys!). I will never forget those days because those were the days that built my faith, when I saw how faithful God was and still is, when everything looked impossible. Those days are what have allowed me to have the love, admiration, and gratitude for each of you today! Thank you for your heart for ministry, your obedience to God's call to support, and for being so faithful and consistent. I truly believe we *will* reach *one billion* souls for Jesus! And I don't mind going into the pit every day. It's a lot easier when I know I have all of you holding the rope! *Thank you!*

ABOUT THE AUTHOR

KELLY K IS a husband, father of five, preacher, teacher, writer, and social media missionary. Preaching the love of Jesus in a manner that is both fresh and passionate, Kelly K is a highly sought-after conference speaker and social media evangelist. Kelly K believes that social media is the largest mission field that the world has ever seen, and his messages reach out to inspire and encourage millions of lives through many multimedia platforms every single day, not just teaching them *about* Jesus but equipping them to go out and *be* the hands and feet of Jesus.

Kelly K's approach to communicating focuses on bridging the gap of cultures, ages, and societies by offering a sound that is relevant to every listener or reader. So many have been blessed by the words, love, and passion of Kelly K, and thousands have come to know Jesus as their personal Lord and Savior every week by him leveraging social media for the Lord. Kelly K currently lives in Kingfisher, Oklahoma, with his beautiful wife, Lindsay. He has five children: Brennen, Jett, Jaxx, Avery, and Chase. He is currently the associate pastor at Limitless Church of Kingfisher.

Pictured from left: Brennen and her husband, Kyle;
Kelly; Jett; Jaxx; Lindsay; Avery; and Chase

CONNECT WITH ME

Follow Kelly K on social media for daily posts, videos, sermons, Bible studies, and more!

 TikTok: @KellyKMinistries

 Facebook.com/KellyKopp13

 @KellyKMinistries

 YouTube.com/KellyKMinistry

Find more books by Kelly K at KellyKMinistries.com, Amazon, and Audible!

To request Kelly K to come and speak at your church or event, please email: info@KellyKMinistries.com.

Support this ministry by texting the word "GIVE" to (209) 242-8899.

linktr.ee/kellykministries